which?
essential guides

BABY AND TODDLER
ESSENTIALS

D0792876

"With so many baby products available, it can be very difficult to decide what you really need. This book helps you work out what you will actually use and how to choose safe products that suit your new lifestyle. **"**

Anne Smith

About the author
Anne Smith currently works as a child safety consultant.
She previously worked for Which? in their research and testing centre and has served on BSI committees for almost 30 years.
She currently chairs the ANEC Child Safety Working Group and represents them on standardisation committees in Europe.
Anne is a mother to three daughters and a grandmother to three.

which? essential guides

BABY AND TODDLER ESSENTIALS

ANNE SMITH

Which? Books are commissioned and published by Which? Ltd,
2 Marylebone Road, London NW1 4DF
Project management for Which? Books: Luke Block
Email: books@which.co.uk

Distributed by Littlehampton Book Services Ltd, Faraday Close, Durrington, Worthing,
West Sussex BN13 3RB

British Library Cataloguing in Publication Data
A catalogue record for this book is available from the British Library

Edited and additional text by: Sean Callery
Designed by: Bob Vickers
Index by: Lynda Swindells
Cover photographs by: Getty Images Ltd
Printed and bound by Scotprint, Scotland

For a full list of Which? Books, please call 01903 828557, access our website at
www.which.co.uk, or write to Littlehampton Book Services.
For other enquiries call 0800 252 100.

Contents

Introduction

Having a baby is a major event in any couple's life and alongside the joy comes understandable concern about getting through the birth, and about being a good parent afterwards. These natural anxieties can trigger a monumental spending spree because the common human reaction to the need to be prepared is to get hold of the necessary equipment.

A massive industry has grown up to meet the need for birthing and baby products. Much of what it produces is useful and some will make a significant improvement to a parent's and baby's quality of life. Other items will join the stack of unnecessary products many households stock, unsullied by use and hidden away under the stairs, probably alongside (choose your own favourites here): the fondue set, the ice cream and bread makers, and that espresso machine that never produced the frothy delights pictured on the packaging.

During pregnancy the tendency is to focus on the birth, rather than the subsequent period when you are coping with being a parent. As a result, the myriad choices (cot or bed, pushchair or buggy, breast or bottle feed, disposables or terry nappies, and so on) can be made in a blurred hurry as you contemplate last night's interrupted sleep and the need to get back home before the next feed is due. This book will help you choose the products that are right for you. Everyone is different and has their own needs and preferences. The trick is to make the right choices first time around so that you don't end up with a pramful of jumble.

❝A massive industry has grown up to meet the need for birthing and baby products. This book helps you choose those that are right for you.❞

 Buying second-hand baby products makes a lot of sense – you save money on items that you may only use for a few months – but you want to be sure it is safe. See pages 197–9 for advice on this.

CHANGING TIMES

The wide range of baby products available today may make decision-making difficult, but it also has its benefits. Forty years ago, for example, baby wipes didn't exist – and nor did baby monitors, changing bags, travel-system pushchairs, disposable nappies or travel cots. There were no car seats: people used to put their babies in carrycots on the back seat of the car. You couldn't get your pram on the bus. New parents bought two dozen terry nappies for their baby, plus plastic pants, safety pins, nappy buckets and special disinfectant; the drying rack and washing line were always full of terry nappies, and preventing nappy rash was a major preoccupation.

Compared with all this, modern baby products are blissfully sophisticated. Pushchairs are multi-functional, light and manageable; nappies are easy for you to deal with and comfortable for your baby, and you also have the option to 'buy green' if that is important to you. Safety standards are vastly improved, and the increased choice in a competitive market can also mean more affordability.

That said, the complexities of modern life – not to mention modern marketing techniques – have resulted in increasing pressure to buy a burgeoning number of 'necessary' baby products. Because we are more mobile, we need equipment that is portable and convenient for travelling about. Working parents, under significant time constraints, are compelled to buy labour- and time-saving devices. In addition, parenting can be a bit of a guilt-trip and it is easy to feel you are doing more for your child if you buy something for him or her. Then there's the 'trend' factor, with fashion-chasing retailers and a media preoccupation with what famous babies are wearing (or riding in) adding to the strain for new parents anxious to give their baby the best start in life.

CHANGING NEEDS

Your and your baby's needs change all the time. As you become used to being a parent, your own priorities evolve. What seemed essential has become redundant, and what appeared to be a luxury will actually come in very handy. Similarly, it can come as quite a shock

❝ You and your baby's needs change all the time. What seemed essential becomes redundant, and what appeared to be a luxury, comes in very handy indeed. ❞

when your baby starts neglecting a favourite plaything, but it is a sign that he or she is growing up, and has new and different needs.

WHAT THIS BOOK CAN DO

This book describes the many different types of product available, gives guidance on their advantages and disadvantages to help you identify what you really need and what you can safely glide the pushchair past. It lists the major manufacturers and retailers, plus many smaller concerns such as independent nursery stores and small-scale manufacturers. Together they provide a wealth of items, some of which are just what you need, and some of which really aren't worth the trouble. It also helps you pick out the most useful sites in the internet minefield, to help you click the most useful button when faced with hundreds of thousands of choices in your search for advice, information or that 'must have' product.

Baby and Toddler Essentials provides new parents − and grandparents − with knowledge and reassurance about what you need and where to get it, at a period in your life when you probably haven't got the energy or time to carry out the thorough research you'd like to do.

" Use *Baby and Toddler Essentials* to decide which of the myriad products that are available to you you really want to buy. "

First essentials

Although baby magazines and retailer catalogues can make you feel that you need an endless array of items for your new baby, you don't. The basics required from day one are nappies, a few changes of clothing, a suitable place for your baby to sleep, and perhaps feeding equipment plus, if you will be travelling by car, a car seat. So don't feel you must rush to buy everything now.

1

Birthing equipment

Even if you opt for a hospital birth, there are many items that can be useful for the big event, and some of them come in very handy during the later stages of pregnancy.

PAIN RELIEF

Whether you plan to give birth in a hospital or at home, you can expect to have access to pain relief from the medical staff, but the TENS (Transcutaneous Electrical Nerve Stimulation) machine may be valuable because it offers pain relief during the late stages of pregnancy (37 weeks and onwards) and during and after childbirth. TENS uses a low-frequency current to stimulate your body's production of natural pain-killing endorphins. Four self-adhesive electrodes are attached to your back and a hand-held button controls the intensity of the current, putting you in control. It is popular because TENS has no effect on the baby or your mental alertness. You won't be able to use it if you are epileptic or have a pacemaker.

SUPPORT PILLOWS

Support pillows support your bump and tummy or knees during pregnancy, helping you to rest and sleep, and can help keep you or your baby comfortable when breast-feeding. Support pillows are usually V-shaped and are also known as maternity or pregnancy pillows. There is more information on these in the section on feeding, pages 80–1.

❝A TENS machine offers valuable pain relief during the later stages of pregnancy and during and after childbirth.❞

 There are specialist suppliers of birth pools - see www.birthworks.co.uk and www.waterbirth.co.uk. For more addresses and telephone numbers, see page 204.

BIRTH POOL

Birth pools can help you relax during pregnancy and during the birth itself (when the warm water and 'supportive' environment provide natural pain relief), and are a warm, comfortable environment to share with your baby in its early life. Hiring is the obvious choice. If you want a home water birth, this is your route, but setting up, filling and emptying the pool requires space, time and effort. A key issue is hygiene: some firms use disposable liners, others go for the less wasteful option of thorough sterilisation of the equipment. There are different sizes of tub available, in wood or plastic, and some models are inflatable (so you would need a pump).

BIRTH BALL

Also known as gym, fitness or exercise balls, these are large inflatable balls for use in ante-and post-natal exercises and during birth. For example, leaning over the ball can ease lower back pain. Check the material is burst resistant so that it will deflate slowly if cut or punctured. Get advice on the size that suits your height, and don't forget you'll need a foot pump to inflate it.

BEAN BAG

A simpler alternative is a large bean bag for achieving a comfortable position during and after labour. This can also provide support when feeding your baby: prop the bag up against a wall for additional stability. It might form part of the family seating arrangements from then on. Handles are useful for moving it around, and make sure the cover is removable for washing.

BED PROTECTORS

If you are planning on giving birth at home, you'll want to protect your mattress from becoming stained. You can achieve this with protective sheets. The most comfortable option is probably one with layers of cotton sandwiching an absorbent polyurethane membrane.

❝ Hygiene is a major issue when using a birthing pool. You can choose between disposable liners or thorough sterilisation of all equipment. ❞

What you need ahead of the birth

It makes sense to equip yourself with these essentials ahead of your due date so that you don't have to issue instructions from your bed for someone to rush to the shops.

Items you will need from day one

- Moses basket, crib, cradle, carrycot or cot (see pages 44-55)

- Mattress and bedding (see pages 56-67)

- Clothing - four to six sleepsuits and bodysuits are sufficient to start off with, plus a couple of cardigans and a hat

- Nappies - a packet of first-size disposables to start off with, or a selection of reusable nappies (see pages 18-20)

- Cotton wool and baby wipes

- A shawl or blanket to wrap your baby in

- Bottles, formula milk and some sort of sterilising equipment (see pages 82-90) if you are bottle-feeding (it's also worth having some bottles and formula even if you are planning to breast-feed - just in case)

- Car seat (see pages 114-22) if you will be travelling by car from day one (including bringing your baby home from hospital)

Items you will need in the first days and weeks

- A pram, a pushchair that is suitable from birth, a travel system or a baby carrier (see pages 128-31 and 140-9)

- A towel for just your baby's use and a gentle baby-bath solution

- Muslin cloths and bibs (see pages 107-9) for spills and dribbles

- A detergent for washing clothes that is suitable for baby's sensitive skin

Other items you may choose to buy

- Scratch mittens (see page 14)
- Changing mat or changing unit (see pages 21 and 68–71)
- Changing bag (see pages 24–5)
- Breast pads, feeding bra and possibly breast pump if you are breast-feeding (see pages 78–81)
- Dummies (see pages 26–7)
- Reclined cradle (see pages 28–30)
- Baby bath or bath supports (but a washing-up bowl in the sink or the main bath will do fine) (see pages 32–5)
- Baby monitor (see pages 36–42)

'Non-baby' items that you will probably be thankful for

- An efficient, reliable washing machine and tumble-drying facility
- A clothes-drying rack if you do not have a tumble-drier
- A microwave for sterilising and/or for heating baby food later on

❝Plan what items you do and don't require before the birth of your baby and then you can relax, safe in the knowledge that you have everything to hand.❞

Clothing

You will probably be inundated with all sorts of baby clothes from friends and relatives so keep your purchases to the minimum. It will soon be clear that some items are more fiddly or difficult to put on your baby than others, and these will be cast to the back of the wardrobe or brought out just for special occasions. If you are buying baby clothes yourself for a newborn, bear the following points in mind.

Sleepsuits, which are all-in-one outfits with built-in feet, are the most practical item to dress your baby in during the early weeks. They are usually made of cotton-jersey or a poly-cotton mix and are very comfortable to wear and easy to wash.

Avoid sleepsuits that have poppers at the back rather than the crotch area, otherwise every time you want to change a nappy you will have to take the whole outfit off. Any item with poppers down the back can be uncomfortable for your baby as he or she will be lying on the seam.

Bodysuits, which are all-in-one vests with a wide neck and poppers at the crotch, are another newborn staple. These are more practical than standard vests as they don't ride up.

Buy some scratch mittens. The skin of new babies can be very sensitive and prone to rashes and their fingernails quite hard. Babies instinctively scratch any irritation. Scratch mittens are simple, thin cotton mittens that help prevent your baby from damaging his or her skin by scratching.

Keep clothes in the 'newborn' size to a minimum, or bypass them altogether – your baby will outgrow these very quickly. Clothes labelled '0–3 months' will last for longer, although they will be a little large at the beginning.

Necklines of jumpers and sweatshirts should have poppers at the side so you are not pulling them over your baby's face to put them on.

❝Choose clothes for your baby that are as simple as possible to put on and take off. Velcro is good, poppers less so.❞

Hand-made cardigans and shawls
should have a fine weave otherwise little
fingers can get caught up in the gaps.
Threaded ribbons or cords should be
avoided as they may become wound
around a baby's neck, and any buttons
should be sewn on securely (see pages
154–65 on safety).

Baby bootees can look cute but are not
necessary, and knitted bootees, in
particular, often fall off – socks are far
more practical.

A snowsuit can be a useful item of
clothing in winter if you are taking your
baby for walks in the pram, but
remember that you don't need layers of
blankets and clothing too. If you buy a
snowsuit, make sure it is easy to take off
or at least undo if you spend time
indoors – for example, in a warm shop.
Buy the snowsuit a size larger than your
baby's normal clothes so that it is not
too constricting.

Many retailers produce 'gift pack'
sets of clothes for newborns. The
chances are that these will include items
that you don't use or find too fancy, so
leave these on the shelf and spend your
money on more practical clothing.

**You may choose to buy clothes in
sales** or when they are on special offer.
This will be fine for basics, such as
bodysuits, but for other clothes it can be
hard to predict what size and style you
will need as the seasons change and
your baby grows.

**You will be handling a mountain of
washing** – some babies can go through
several outfits a day – so any clothing
you buy should be suitable for machine
washing. Hand-wash- and dry-clean-only
garments are definitely a bad idea, unless
they are for a special occasion.

You should wash all items of clothing
in a detergent that is suitable for a baby's
sensitive skin before using them.

❝ Avoid threaded
ribbons or cords as
they can easily become
wound around your
baby's neck. ❞

For more information on shopping for clothes, see Where to shop on pages 186–95.

Nappies

Packets of nappies are likely to be taking up space in your shopping trolley for years to come. If you opt for disposables – as most parents do – you will be buying them for two-and-a-half to three years from the birth of your baby.

With nappies (and their contents) becoming part of your daily life for so long, you will want to make sure you are choosing the right one for your baby. Babies come in all shapes and sizes, and there may be some trial and error involved in finding a nappy you are happy with.

❝ Modern disposable nappies are highly absorbent and are made in a range of sizes from tiny ones for premature babies to extra-large and 'junior' sizes. ❞

DISPOSABLE NAPPIES

Modern disposable nappies work well at absorbing liquid because they contain a highly absorbent material called polyacrylates. This is trapped inside the nappy layers and can absorb many times its own weight in liquid. When polyacrylates get wet they turn into a gel, holding in the wetness in the process (if a wet nappy splits, the gel is clearly visible).

Kimberly-Clark, maker of Huggies, and Proctor & Gamble, maker of Pampers, are the main manufacturers of disposables; you will find these brands almost everywhere. Most supermarkets also produce own-brand nappies.

Nappies come in a range of sizes, from tiny ones for premature or low-birth weight babies to extra-large and 'junior' sizes. Not all manufacturers use the same sizing categories (although 'mini', 'midi', 'maxi', 'maxi plus' and 'junior' are the most common), but they do label the

The question of disposables versus washables is addressed on pages 20-1.

nappies with the weight range they are designed for, so it is not hard to tell which size you should be buying. The larger the size, the fewer nappies there (usually) are in the packet.

Some manufacturers produce both standard and luxury, or premium, versions of their nappies. Both are very absorbent but the more expensive 'premium' range have extras, such as a softer, cotton feel and an elasticated waistband.

How to choose

You may well experiment with two or three brands before you settle on a favourite, or you may stick with the first brand you buy. Either way, there are certain considerations you should be aware of.

A good disposable nappy should fit well with no gaps; be easy and quick to fasten, open and refasten; and should stay closed without the fastener losing its grip or tearing the nappy.

Use the weight of your baby as a guide but choose the smallest nappy your baby can comfortably wear – a size even slightly too big can be prone to leaks – but make sure you move up to the next size when the nappy starts to seem a bit tight.

Don't go straight for a nappy that is advertised as being super-absorbent. Unless you buy a very basic and cheap brand, in which case inferior absorbency will probably be an issue, most nappies on the market should be able to cope successfully with your baby's output as long as you change the nappy regularly.

 You can save money by buying a cheaper brand of nappy for daytime use and a super-absorbent one for night-time when your baby will be wearing the nappy for longer.

Try out a standard supermarket own-brand nappy or a non-premium type of one of the big brands – you will probably be satisfied with the absorbency.

Nappy features

Manufacturers continually proclaim new developments in comfort, fit and absorbency of their disposable nappies. Some features may well help to keep your baby dry and more comfortable or make things easier for you when you are changing the nappy. Extras such as stretchy sides, a 'breathable' cotton-feel outer layer, Velcro fasteners (as opposed to reusable sticky tape) that won't lose their sticking power if you get nappy cream or talc on them, and effective waist- and leg-leak barriers have their appeal. You will pay a bit extra, of course, but you may decide that such features are well worth having.

Cost cutting

Nappies are going to be one of your major ongoing expenses. Here is how to ease the pain.

- Buy the largest packs to reduce costs but be wary of bulk-buying too much in one size (especially newborn size) as your baby may outgrow them sooner than you expect.
- Take advantage of special offers if you don't have a strong loyalty to one particular brand. Such is the competition between nappy manufacturers that offers are often available.
- Supermarkets and shops selling a range of nappy brands often make it much easier for you to compare prices between brands by displaying the price per nappy alongside the pack price.

WASHABLE NAPPIES

Washable nappies have undergone a transformation in recent years. Traditional terry nappies, with their accompanying folding techniques and safety pins, although still available, are used far less these days. There is nothing wrong with terry nappies – they are the cheapest nappies, wash well and one size fits all – but more modern materials, fashions and lifestyles have changed the way that washable nappies are designed. These days, a baby in a washable nappy is likely to be wearing a soft, cotton, fitted nappy and cover with Velcro or popper fastenings and elasticated waist and legs. The nappies can look very much like disposables and can be put on and taken off just as easily; the only difference being that you wash them rather than throw them away. They last well: you are unlikely to need to buy another set for a second baby.

How to choose

If you are new to the concept of fitted, washable nappies, the wide range of brands and types available can be confusing. You can get catalogues from specialist nappy companies, which include everything from organic knitted tie-on nappies to towelling booster pads for extra absorbency. The basic choice, however, is between two-piece and one-piece nappies.

Two-piece nappies consist of the nappy itself – which is usually made from cotton terry towelling or flannel, often with an element of polyester – and a separate outer wrap, which tends to be made from polyester with a waterproof layer. The nappies are shaped to fit and no folding is required, although you can also buy 'prefolds',

❝ To reduce costs, buy the largest packs, take advantage of special offers and compare the prices per nappy. ❞

which are flat nappies partly sewn into shape to make folding easier. These are held in place with safety pins or special plastic 'grippers'.

The outer wrap and usually the nappy itself do up with either poppers or Velcro. The wrap gives extra security from leaks and keeps everything in its place. Although the nappies need to be washed after each use, the wraps don't, unless they have been soiled.

One-piece nappies are similar to two-piece ones, but have an integral waterproof outer layer. They are quicker to put on and take off but they can be more difficult to keep clean and take longer to dry.

In addition to the one-piece or two-piece nappies, you can buy extra liners for times when additional absorbency is needed – night-time or travelling, for instance. Washable or disposable (and biodegradable) liners are available. Many people use liners on a daily basis – they can make nappy changes simpler because you can dispose of the liner and flush the solids away and keep the nappy itself going.

> **❝ Buy extra liners for times when additional absorbency is needed, such as at night-time or when travelling. ❞**

Looking after washable nappies

Although they can be tumble-dried, if you are buying washable nappies for environmental reasons (see page 20), be aware that air-drying is more environmentally friendly. However, nappies can take several hours to dry, depending on the type, so you need to make sure you have the space and the spares to allow for this. Soaking prior to washing is recommended, so be prepared to live with nappy buckets that are full of soiled nappies.

If all that is too much trouble but you still want to use washable nappies, there are locally run nappy washing services that will collect, launder and return them – at a price.

Washables work out cheaper than disposables, especially if you use traditional terry nappies rather than the more modern, fitted-style washable nappies. If you choose washable nappies, you will be paying more at the outset, but in the long run, costs will be lower, especially if you use the nappies again for subsequent children.

The main disadvantage with washables, of course, is that you have to soak and wash them. In addition, washable nappies can be less absorbent *Dispos @ night?* than disposables so people find that they need to change them more often than with disposables. Some parents will use both washables and disposables so that they gain some of the advantages of both – perhaps using disposables when going out for the day or on holiday, and washables at other times.

19

Where to buy washable nappies

If you are going to be using washable nappies, it is recommended that you buy 20–30 nappies and four wraps. Washables are widely available these days and nursery stores such as Mothercare do sell them, but you are likely to find a much larger selection and more information from one of the many specialist mail-order or online nappy firms and nappy networks (see pages 208–9). Take advantage of trial packs offered by manufacturers if you are not sure of which brand to buy – rather than make the expensive mistake of buying a bulk-load of nappies you are not happy with.

❝ It is estimated that a baby gets through around 5,000 nappies before he or she is toilet trained. ❞

DISPOSABLES VERSUS WASHABLES

Disposables are undoubtedly more convenient as you just throw them away after use – hence their huge popularity. They don't contribute towards your washing and are slim and light, so you can easily carry several around with you when you are out and about. A major disadvantage, however, is their cost. During the first few months you can expect to be changing a nappy about six times a day, which is roughly 40 a week, or 160 per month. Even though the cost of each individual nappy is low, it certainly mounts up over time.

Nappies and the environment

Disposable nappies have a significant environmental impact. Apart from the energy and materials used in their production, environmental organisations express concern that the widespread use of disposables is producing vast quantities of waste that could take hundreds of years to decompose. It is estimated that a baby will get through around 5,000 nappies before he or she is toilet trained. Consequently, approximately eight billion nappies enter the waste stream every year in the UK, and the vast majority of them end up in landfill sites where parts

If you want advice from other parents on reusable nappies, look at the cloth nappies chat forum on parenting websites such as www.ukparents.co.uk. This site also operates a buy-and-sell forum for washable nappies.

of each nappy will take 200 years or more to decompose. Nappies make up at least 4 per cent of all household waste. The disposal of nappies is estimated to cost each local authority up to £500,000 a year – so local authorities, as well as environmental pressure groups, have a particular incentive to see this waste reduced.

Disposable nappies undeniably cause more waste than washable nappies, but washable nappies have their own environmental impact, albeit in different ways. Washing nappies at home means you use extra energy and water to keep them clean – resources you don't need to use with disposables. If you wash at high temperatures and use a tumble-drier this increases the energy used. Manufacturers of disposables highlight this to defend the comparative environmental impact of disposables.

Both environmental organisations and disposable nappy manufacturers have produced their own studies, but the independent consensus is that there is, as yet, no clear answer as to which type of nappy is most environmentally friendly overall. However, because much of the environmental impact of washable nappies occurs during their use, parents can be proactive in minimising this:

- Use an economical wash cycle and line- or air-dry rather than tumble-dry.
- Make sure the nappies get passed on to other babies.
- A nappy laundry service can be the greenest option.

" Disposable nappies undeniably cause more waste than washable nappies, but washable nappies have their own environmental impact. "

NAPPY ACCESSORIES
You will find some accessories far more useful to you than others, so it makes sense to buy small quantities of these items at first, then bulk buy what is actually going to make your and your baby's life better.

Changing mats
You can change your baby on a towel, but a changing mat is a relatively inexpensive item that can make nappy changing a bit easier. For one thing, it has a waterproof, wipe-clean plastic covering so that those inevitable 'little accidents' can be easily cleaned up. Avoid changing mats with a towelling rather than a plastic covering – they may be more comfortable on your baby's bottom but you will probably end up washing the cover more often than you would wish (if you are really anxious about that cold bottom, you can put a towel on top of a standard changing mat anyway).

Changing mats are padded and they have slightly raised sides so that when your baby starts to squirm around it is more difficult for him or her to wriggle off the mat. There are also inflatable models that blow up to form high sides.

21

If you get a changing bag (see pages 24–5), it will probably include a 'travel' changing mat. These can be useful when you are out and about. Nappy manufacturers have come up with disposable changing mats. There is no point in getting one of these if you already have a portable changing mat, and even if you don't, they are one more item in the long list of baby products you can easily do without.

What is the age?

> ‎‎❝ When you baby is newborn, cotton wool and warm water will usually be adequate for keeping his or her bottom clean. ❞

> **!** The floor is the safest place to change your baby. Even if you have the mat on a changing table (see pages 68-71), you should always keep your baby within your reach in case he or she wriggles off. If you change your baby on the floor, be particularly careful if you have older children playing nearby.

Baby wipes

You will be buying these for as long as your baby is using nappies. Wipes are basically soft cloth or paper rectangles impregnated with a moist cleansing formula. When your baby is newborn, cotton wool and warm water will usually be adequate for keeping his or her bottom clean, but you will be looking for something more efficient before long. Wipes normally come in oblong plastic packets with feed-through lids so you can pull the wipes out with one hand; for a small extra cost you can buy these packets in a plastic storage container, also with a feed-through lid.

Extra features that may appeal include 'built-in' baby lotion, extra-soft material or fragrance-free cleanser. There are significant price differences between supermarket own-brands and big-brand names. Try the own-brands first: you could find that they suit your needs perfectly well.

Nappy sacks

These are mini-plastic bags that are designed to enable you to dispose of your nappies hygienically. You take the nappy off your baby, put it in the bag and then in the bin or somewhere else in preparation for disposal. The bags are effective at masking the smell of a dirty nappy, but some parents find

⬇ See pages 208-9 of Useful addresses for information on specialist companies that sell nappies and disposal units.

the overpowering chemical aroma of nappy sacks almost as bad as the nappy itself. You could also use a standard plastic grocery bag tied up at the handles.

Disposal units and nappy buckets

If you use disposable nappies and really don't like the idea of having soiled nappies lurking in a bin in the house before they get thrown out, you can buy special nappy disposal 'units'. The nappy is placed in the unit and is automatically sealed into a plastic sleeve. You end up with a long string of sealed nappy parcels that you throw away when the unit is full.

If you use reusable nappies, you will need to have a nappy bucket for soaking soiled nappies. It should have a secure lid, an easy-to-use handle for when you need to empty the contents, and preferably a pouring lip. You can buy nappy buckets from nursery stores or specialist reusable nappy mail-order companies (see box, below left).

❝ A nappy bucket should have a secure lid and an easy-to-use handle. ❞

Nappies and nappy rash

There is evidence to suggest that modern, highly absorbent disposable nappies can help prevent nappy rash because the urine is absorbed, keeping the skin dry. If you use washable nappies, you need to make sure they are properly cleaned and rinsed, as traces of ammonia or detergent may be left behind, which can then trigger nappy rash. Using a nappy sanitiser when you soak the nappies should help reduce the likelihood of this.

Whatever type of nappy you use and however you look after your baby's bottom, a key way to help prevent nappy rash is to change the nappy regularly.

& let skin breathe sometimes

Changing bags

New parents often regard a changing bag as a 'must have' item. These bags do have advantages – for example, wipe-clean compartments that are just the right size for nappies, bottles and other baby essentials, and a portable changing mat.

When you are getting to grips with all the extra organisation involved in taking a baby out for an afternoon, a handy bag designed specifically for baby paraphernalia is one thing that can help the day run smoothly (as long as you keep it stocked up, that is).

Having said that, it's not as if an ordinary, relatively roomy bag can't do the job of carrying your baby's things. Any bag that can hold a few nappies and wipes, a bottle or two, a change of baby clothes and a travel changing mat, plus a few of your own bits and pieces, will do just fine. How necessary a changing bag is depends on whether you are a minimalist parent who likes to stick to the bare essentials or whether you like the idea of the full baby kit.

Changing bags are widely available. Style-wise, you can choose from shoulder bags or rucksacks or a bag that can convert into a soft carrier (see box, below opposite).

" A handy bag designed specifically for baby paraphernalia is one thing that can help the day run smoothly. "

Points to consider before buying: Changing bags

This changing bag is going to be an important part of your life! These guidelines will help you choose one that suits you.

Choose a bag that is washable as it is bound to get grubby.

Check that the straps seem secure and the bag appears durable – you'll be hauling it around on a daily basis so you don't want the straps hanging off by the third month.

You don't need countless internal compartments and pockets – this makes it easier to lose track of what you've put where, which can be highly irritating when, for example, you need some wipes in a hurry. In many ways, the simpler the bag, the better.

Some bags have large bottle-insulating compartments – these are potentially useful for bottle-fed babies, but are not necessary if you are breast-feeding.

Rucksack-style bags have an advantage in that they are less likely to get in your way – and you will be less tempted to hang it on the handles of the pram or pushchair (see page 151).

If both you and your partner will be using the bag when out and about, you may want to choose a unisex design – there are lots of sporty styles.

If you like to keep your own things separate but in the same bag, some bags have special pockets for storing your own items, such as a mobile phone or loose change.

“ Choose a bag that is washable and has secure and durable looking straps. You don't need too many internal compartments – the simpler the bag, the better. ”

For more information on soft carriers, see Baby carriers on pages 128-31.

Dummies

These are called soothers in Europe and pacifiers in America, and can provoke all sorts of emotions. Some parents hate the idea of their child having a dummy - often for aesthetic reasons as much as anything - and would prefer that a thumb or finger is sucked. Others come to regard the dummy as their saviour (woe betide the parent who forgets the favourite dummy on a long car journey or day trip).

Babies themselves often have strong preferences. Some babies seem to have a clear need for 'non-nutritive' sucking. The comfort provided by the dummy can become addictive – you can be sure that if social embarrassment and parental pressure to give up had not taken effect by the post-toddler stage, some children would happily go to school with a dummy in their bag. Other babies simply don't like dummies, no matter how keen their parents are for them to have one.

❝Some babies simply don't like dummies, no matter how keen their parents may be for them to have one. ❞

TYPES OF DUMMY

As with teats for bottles (see page 85), dummy teats are made from either latex or silicone mounted on a plastic shield. Silicone teats are preferable from a parent's point of view. They don't have the rubbery smell of latex, which you may notice if your baby is an ardent sucker of a latex dummy. On the other hand, babies themselves often prefer latex because it is more flexible and softer to suck. If you plan to give your baby a dummy, try a silicone teat first and move on to rubber if necessary.

The shape of the teat may also be an issue. You can buy dummies with either an orthodontic teat or a traditional bell-shaped teat. If you are not confident that you will be able to limit your baby's dummy use to the first few months (before he or she develops a set of teeth), try an orthodontic teat first as these are designed to cause the least disturbance to the developing teeth. If your baby prefers a bell shape, however, it is nothing to panic about. Thumb-sucking is more of an issue when it comes to teeth because you can't take your baby's thumb away.

Points to consider include:

- **Buy several at a time.** Dummies get lost easily so it is always worth having a few spares.
- **Some brands come in plastic containers.** These are handy for keeping your dummies clean.
- **You can buy dummy chains,** with clips that attach to your baby's clothing at one end and to the dummy at the other end – these are useful if your baby is constantly dropping his or her dummy.
- Check the condition of dummies regularly and throw away any that are damaged or appear to be worn.
- Sterilise young babies' dummies regularly (see pages 87–90).

 It is important to note that babies and toddlers should not be given dummies dipped in sugary drinks, fruit juices or honey as there is well-documented evidence to suggest this practice can cause tooth decay in infant teeth (see also page 98).

Dummy safety

- To reduce the risk of choking, make sure the dummy is made from a single moulded piece with holes stamped out.
- Always check over the dummy nipple – if it becomes brittle, it could break up and become a choking risk.
- Never tie a dummy around a child's neck, for risk of strangulation.

❝ Check the condition of dummies regularly and throw away any that are damaged or appear to be worn. ❞

Reclined cradles

You can get a lot of use out of a reclined cradle during the first few months (you should stop using it when your baby can sit). It provides a safe place for parking a wide-awake baby when you have both hands busy with other tasks.

Sessions in the chair can give your baby a change of scene and, because seated and harnessed in at a slant, he or she can watch you as you do whatever you are doing. Some chairs are more padded than others and have a reclined position so you can use them as an extra dozing place (although they are not really suitable for lengthy sessions because they do not provide the same support as a cot or a pram). Others have a simpler design. All can also be used as a feeding chair when your baby is being weaned but is too young for the highchair.

> **A reclined cradle can be used as a feeding chair when your baby is being weaned but is too young for the highchair.**

TYPES OF RECLINED CRADLE

Although there are variations within each category, there are three main types of reclined cradle: wire-framed, padded tubular and automated, while a further option is an automatic baby swing. See the table opposite for the pros and cons of each of the following types.

Wire-framed cradles

This is the simplest style. Fabric is stretched around a wire frame, which is at a reclining angle and curves round to a flat base. You can gently bounce the cradle by jigging the frame.

Padded, tubular-framed cradles

More luxurious than the wire-framed models, these usually have adjustable lie-back positions as well as extra padding. They are fairly sturdy and have a more rounded appearance than the wire-framed type. Some models have carrying handles and you can often adjust the cradle to have either a fixed or rocking base.

Automated cradles

These are really a cross between a reclined cradle and an automatic baby swing. You can normally opt to have them in the standard bouncy chair mode or in the vibrating mode, which is meant to gently simulate the vibrations of a car engine. The vibrations are battery-powered and you can adjust the speed.

 Never place a bouncy cradle on a raised surface such as a table-top. One unexpected lurch forward from your baby could send him or her flying or skidding off and could cause serious injury. For the same reason, never place a cradle outside next to a paddling pool or garden pond.

The pros and cons of different types of cradle

Wire-framed cradles

Pros	Cons
• The least expensive type • Basic style but perfectly adequate for its purpose • Light and easy to move around the house	• No recline position and little or no padding, so may be less comfortable for your baby if he or she wants to snooze • Non-folding so difficult to put away out of sight

Padded, tubular-framed cradles

Pros	Cons
• Versatile because of features such as the adjustable lie-back • Rounded sides and more cradle-like shape so may help your baby feel more secure • Fold-flat models available	• More expensive than the wire-framed version • You may not use the extra features, for which you are paying more

Automated cradles

Pros	Cons
• Vibrating motion can be an effective soother – if you have to take the car out to get your baby to sleep, an automated cradle could be a convenient alternative • Not necessarily more expensive than the non-automated types	• Vibrating motion may well be an unnecessary extra – most babies will be perfectly happy with the standard manual bounce and some may even dislike the vibrations • Extra noise caused by the vibrations may be irritating

Points to consider before buying: Reclined cradles

The following advice will help you make the right choice for you.

If you are buying a travel system (see pages 144-6), a reclined cradle will almost certainly be included.

If your baby seems happy using the infant car seat (see pages 114-22) as an indoor seat, especially if it is a seat with a rocking motion, a reclined cradle will probably be unnecessary.

Some models have removable, washable seat covers (as opposed to sponge-clean) - these are much more practical if you are likely to use the cradle as a feeding chair at some time.

Reclined cradles can take up space - look for a fold-flat model if you mind the idea of it as a semi-permanent fixture.

Some reclined cradles come with toy bars, which can provide added entertainment value for your baby; alternatively, you can simply position a baby gym over the cradle.

A head-support cushion is included with many models - this can be useful for very young babies.

Padding is not a crucial feature - cradles without padding still provide adequate support.

Because you will only be using the cradle for a few months it may be worth bypassing the more expensive end of the market.

"If space is an issue at home, look for a fold-flat reclined cradle so that it can be put away when your baby isn't using it. "

 If your baby has enjoyed lying in a reclined cradle, he or she might like to move on to a baby bouncer or walker: see pages 172-6.

AUTOMATIC BABY SWINGS

These comprise a padded chair or swing on a rigid metal or plastic frame. They are battery-operated; turn them on and your baby swings gently without your having to lift a finger. Some come with extras such as a play tray with toys and music that plays while the swing is in motion. Baby swings are usually suitable for babies from birth to 11kg (24lb 4oz) (about ten months) and are widely available in nursery stores.

> **" A baby swing provides you with an extra place to 'park' your baby and gives him or her a bit of variety. "**

The pros and cons of automatic baby swings

Pros	Cons
• Can soothe many babies to sleep (they also have a reputation for calming colicky babies)	• Quite expensive for an item that will only be in use for a few months (nine to ten at the most) and which your baby may not even like
• Provide an extra place for you to 'park' your baby and give him or her a bit of variety	• It would take up a lot of space in the living room

Baby baths

During the early weeks, a baby bath enables you to bathe your baby without having to stoop over the main bath and allows you to wash your baby in a room other than the bathroom. Bathing your baby in the living room next to a warm fire, or in your bedroom or the nursery, may be more convenient and cosier than in a chilly bathroom.

However, a baby bath is not a necessity. Many parents like to have a bath with their baby – the skin-to-skin contact this provides can be a pleasant experience for both baby and parent. You can bathe your baby in the kitchen sink lined with a towel or foam bath support (see overleaf) for comfort or use a washing-up bowl. As long as the washing-up is cleared away and the surfaces are clean, the sink serves as a convenient, waist-height bathing platform. Newborn babies do not actually need to have a complete bath for a couple of weeks or so, anyway. Instead, you can opt to 'top and tail' them – you just need two small bowls of warm water and some cotton wool for washing the face/upper body and bottom separately. Or you can buy 'top and tail' bowls with two separate compartments in one bowl.

The lifespan of a baby bath may be fairly short – by the time your baby is a month or two old, a standard baby bath may well be too small and the splashes too large to make it useful. But for the brief period before this, a baby bath can be a helpful, if non-essential, item to have. Other bath products (see overleaf)

are used in different ways and may have a longer lifespan. If you have a changing unit (see pages 68–71), this may come with a baby bath, so you won't need to buy a separate one.

❝ A baby bath is not a must have, but it can be helpful. ❞

TYPES OF BABY BATH

There is a choice of simple, oval-shaped baths or baths with a slightly angled shape for extra ease of handling and support. Whichever sort you go for, a slip-resistant textured base is an important feature (soapy babies are notoriously slippery). You should also check that the bath is sturdy and made of firm moulded plastic with no sharp or rough edges – cheap, thin plastic can bow with the weight of the water. A drainage hole and plug can be helpful for emptying the water, but are not essential. Easy-to-grip sides or handles are, however, because you may be moving the bath around when it is full of water. For the pros and cons of baby baths, see opposite.

Standard baby baths

These can be used anywhere, in the main bath or anywhere else in the house (even outside in the garden on warm days).

Rest-on-rim baths

These are baby baths with either a very wide rim or supports at either end, designed so that you can rest them on

the rim of the main bath. They should have a plug-hole so you can empty the water out easily.

Bucket baths

Shaped like a large bucket, these are designed so your baby is washed in a sitting or foetal position rather than a lying position.

The pros and cons of baby baths

Standard baby baths

Pros	Cons
• Can be placed on a secure table or bed so you can work at a comfortable height • Small babies may feel more secure in the compact shape of a baby bath	• Take up a fair amount of storage space for something with such a short lifespan

Rest-on-rim baths

Pros	Cons
• Your baby is positioned at a convenient kneeling height so you don't have to bend right over the bath • Can also be used as a stand-alone bath	• More expensive than standard baths • Same lifespan and storage restrictions as standard baths • If your main bath is a non-standard shape or size, the rest-on-rim bath might not fit

Bucket baths

Pros	Cons
• Small babies may feel more secure being bathed in the foetal position • Use less water and space than conventional baby baths • Easier shape to carry when full • Water stays warm for longer	• Same limited lifespan as conventional baths – they are recommended for babies up to six months, but a chubby, lively pre-six-month-old may well find the bath constricting • Limited space for playing with bath toys or for being swished around

OTHER BATH ACCESSORIES

You don't need a lot of equipment at bathtime, but the following items can have their uses.

Bath supports

A variety of different products come into this category, all working in roughly the same way. Your baby is normally bathed in the main bath but lies on some sort of soft pad so his or her body is not fully immersed but can still be easily washed. The baby's head is supported above the water line. Products range from simple foam supports to floating polystyrene-filled bathing pads and contoured bath chairs.

Hooded baby towels

These hooded, cape-shaped towels, or 'cuddle robes', are a bit gimmicky. Babies look cute in them (they often have children's character motifs on the hood) and the hood may help keep them warm – but a soft fluffy towel can do the job just as well or better.

Tap cover

Although not an issue with younger babies, once they start pulling themselves up and moving around independently in the bath, there is a risk they could slip or tumble and bang their head against the taps (particularly if you have another child in the bath, too). Some toddlers also have a fascination with trying to turn on the hot tap. One option is to cover the taps with a wet towel. Alternatively, you can buy an inflatable cover which stops children touching the taps and that can also double up as a bath pillow if you relocate it using the suckers.

" A tap cover provides welcome protection from a potentially banged head or scalded body. "

The pros and cons of bath supports	
Pros	Cons
• Comfortable for your baby, particularly the soft supports	• Your baby may not have the freedom to wriggle and splash as in a normal bath and you won't be able to swish him or her around in the same way
• Your hands are free to concentrate on washing	
• Your baby may feel happier not being fully immersed	• Foam supports in particular need to be taken out of the bath and squeeze-dried carefully to prevent mildew developing
• Easy to store; light and compact enough for travel	

Bath thermometer

Running a warm bath for your baby shouldn't be a complicated procedure requiring extra technical equipment. You can test the heat of the bath with the time-honoured method of sticking your elbow or wrist in the water and trusting your instinct. For extra safety you should run the cold tap first followed by the hot. If you feel especially anxious, however, a bath thermometer will reassure you. The ideal temperature is 37°C – which is comfortably warm but not hot. You can also buy bath mats and plugs that change colour when the water is too hot.

Baby toiletries

The wealth of baby toiletry products available is staggering. From standard chain-store own-brand baby shampoos to relatively pricey washes and moisturisers – containing extracts of everything from milk proteins to lavender and camomile oils – the baby-beauty market is big business. Of course, the fancier products appeal more to the personal tastes of parents rather than having any demonstrable benefit over cheaper alternatives, unless a skin condition such as eczema is involved, in which case a specific product may be recommended. Ask you GP or local chemist for advice.

Keep it simple

When it comes to the practicalities of washing your baby and looking after his or her skin, you really don't need much and it is usually a case of the simpler the better. Bear the following in mind.

- **For most babies,** a bottle of simple baby bath is all you will need. Shampooing isn't actually necessary until they are a few weeks old.
- **Newborn babies** don't need any bath products at all – warm water is sufficient.
- **Talcum powder** is, arguably, an unnecessary product whatever the baby's age – make sure you dry him or her properly and see whether this suffices before starting to use it.
- **If your baby's skin** seems dry, a touch of mild, unperfumed baby lotion or moisturiser may help, or you can put a couple of drops of olive oil in the bath. If the dryness seems to be irritating your baby, try an emollient such as Oilatum in the bath. This is more expensive than standard products but you may be able to get it free on prescription if you visit your GP.
- **Don't bother with toiletry** 'gift' or 'starter' packs where you get a selection of different toiletries – you're unlikely to find much use for more than one or two of the bottles in the pack.

Safety with water and in the bathroom are very real issues with babies and toddlers. See 'drowning' on page 156 and more bath and bathing accessories on page 163-4.

Baby monitors

Parents fall into two main camps when it comes to monitors: those who regard them as an indispensable piece of baby equipment and those who can't see any reason to have one at all.

The purpose of a baby monitor is to allow you to hear your baby crying when you are in another part of the house or in the garden. It can be a useful device to have if you are concerned that you won't hear your baby's cries. A few new parents, however, can become preoccupied with the supposed value of their monitor, keeping a close watch on it and listening out for every snuffle and grunt as confirmation that their baby is still breathing. But monitors are not safety devices and, although you can get devices that monitor breathing, healthy babies do not need to be monitored in this way. A monitor should be regarded as a device for parents' convenience.

As part of the baby-product buying bonanza that prospective parents often feel under pressure to engage in, monitors have achieved a degree of 'must have' status. But you don't need one if you can hear your baby crying when you are in the house or flat, and keeping doors open may be a cheaper way of ensuring you can hear your baby. There is also an argument that monitors can encourage parents to over-pamper. Babies will often cry and fuss for a short time then settle themselves back to sleep, but parents who rush to soothe their baby at the merest whimper could contribute towards future sleeping problems. Some monitors can be set so that only the real cries are transmitted – a handy option once anxious parents become more relaxed.

That said, many parents find a monitor to be extremely handy. If you have a pet and need to keep bedroom doors firmly closed, for example, it keeps your baby within earshot. Even if you find you don't need to use it every day, it can have valuable occasional uses – for example, if you are having friends round for a drink and a chat and you want to know above the din that your baby is settled, or if you need to do some work in the garden and you are out of earshot, a portable monitor (beware: some must be plugged into a socket and are not portable) will let you keep tabs on your baby.

If you are deaf or hard-of-hearing, a monitor – particularly one that has a visual display (see overleaf) – will have clear benefits.

❝ A monitor can be extremely handy, even if you don't use it every day. ❞

TYPES OF MONITOR

All monitors are made up of two units. You keep one unit with you or near you and the other next to the baby. The unit next to the baby transmits to your unit, via radio waves (you will usually have a choice of two channels so you can switch if there is interference on one), any sounds he or she makes. The usual operating range is 100 metres. Most can be either mains or battery operated; some have rechargeable batteries. Some models need to be plugged into a socket and have no battery-power facility. See below for the pros and cons of each of the following types.

Mains-powered monitors

These can be plugged into a socket in any room but cannot be used with batteries. They are the simplest type of monitor.

Portable, dual-powered monitors

These run on either the mains or batteries, so the parent unit can be carried around with you when on battery power – some come with a belt clip so you don't need to hold it. The more expensive models in this category have rechargeable batteries.

The pros and cons of monitors

Mains-powered monitors

Pros	Cons
• The least expensive option • Ideal for parents who won't be moving around the house much while the monitor is on, or if they are only likely to be using the monitor at night	• Less versatile because you can't use batteries, so can't be used away from a socket

Portable, dual-powered monitors

Pros	Cons
• Useful for parents who will be busying themselves about the house or garden while the baby is asleep • Rechargeable models are easy to recharge and save you worrying about batteries running out	• More expensive than mains-powered models • You may find you don't use the portable facility enough to justify the extra expense • If you regularly run a non-rechargeable model on batteries, you could find the extra cost of batteries a burden

EXTRA FEATURES

The more you pay for your monitor, the more sophisticated the features are likely to be. Some of these have greater potential use than others.

Visual light display

This is one of the more useful extra features. It allows you to turn off the sound, and a sound-activated multi-light display panel shows whether or not your baby is crying. The louder your baby cries, the more lights are illuminated. If you don't want to hear your baby's every snuffle while you are sitting down to relax, a light display could be handy. It could also be useful in a situation when, for example, you have friends round or are having a meeting with someone at home and you don't want your baby's fussing to disturb things.

Nightlight on baby unit

This gives the area around the unit a soft glow, which may be of comfort to your baby and can help you to see him or her better in a darkened room. If you have this feature on your monitor, you are unlikely to want a separate nightlight as well; however, depending on the intensity of the light, it may be too soft to be much use.

Volume warning

Some monitor models will vibrate to warn you if you have the volume on your unit too low.

Temperature display

A temperature sensor on the baby unit tells you the temperature of the room. If you are worried about controlling the temperature in your baby's room, however, you can buy a cheap nursery thermometer (see page 62) instead of choosing a monitor for this extra feature. Bear in mind here, though, that your baby's temperature is not being monitored – a straightforward and effective way of checking whether your baby is too hot or cold is by feeling his or her stomach.

ff With such a wide choice of potential extra features, decide on what you do and don't want in advance of shopping. **yy**

For more consumer advice about baby monitors, go to the Which? website at www.which.co.uk.

Lullaby trigger

A soothing lullaby is automatically activated if your baby stirs. The effectiveness of this will depend on the individual baby and it has the potential to be more irritating than soothing.

Out-of-range alarm

If you wander out of range, an alarm sounds. This could be useful as a means of helping you assess how far down the garden you can go, but it is hard to see how it would be useful again once you have found this out, unless you are particularly absent-minded.

Multi-channel options

Two channels should be adequate for most people, but if you live in a busy, built-up area with lots of other parents with monitors in close proximity, creating the likelihood of regular interference, the option of more channels may be helpful.

Digital technology

Some models have microprocessors designed to ensure that the only nursery sounds you will be able to hear are those from your own nursery, not anyone

else's. However, this doesn't stop the transmissions from your own monitor being picked up by somebody else.

Two-way talk-back

You can use the parent's unit to talk to your child. This means you can make soothing noises to your baby if he or she starts to wake up and (probably of greater use) you can talk to an older child who has trouble settling down at bedtime.

Long range

Some monitors transmit further than the standard 100 metres. Although this may seem a useful feature in theory, in practice it is not such a good idea to be this far away from your baby. Remember that range is considerably reduced within the home.

 Monitors with cords must never be placed in the cot because of the risk of the cord becoming wound around the baby's neck.

BREATHING AND MOVEMENT MONITORS

A small number of monitors are designed to check for breathing and movement as well as noise. A sensor pad is placed under the mattress to monitor these signs of life. Monitors like this are not considered by everyone to be a good idea. The Foundation for the Study of Infant Deaths (FSID, see box, below) says that healthy babies don't need to be monitored in this way and that there is no evidence this kind of monitoring can prevent cot death. An alarm sounds if there is no movement detected for 15–20 seconds, but there are situations when a baby could stop breathing but still be moving: if he or she is choking, for example.

If a baby does stop breathing and the alarm sounds, parents or carers would need to know resuscitation techniques (a video on this may be included with the monitor). There is also an argument that monitors like these can feed parents' insecurities about cot death and make putting a healthy baby to sleep an unnecessarily anxious time, and there is also the risk of false alarms.

If you are worried about cot death, you should talk to your doctor or health visitor first rather than make a beeline for one of these monitors.

VIDEO MONITORS

You can watch your baby's every move 'live' on your television or on a separate mini-screen on the parent unit. These monitors have a small camera that you position to view your baby. When they are linked to the TV screen you can normally set them to an automatic mode so, if you are watching television and your baby starts to cry, your TV viewing is interrupted so you can see your baby and judge whether you need to go and tend to him or her. The camera has a wide-angled lens and can transmit pictures in the dark. Pictures are in black and white or colour, depending on the model. Such monitors are most definitely at the luxury end of the market but they have the potential to be useful later on when you may need to keep an eye on a mischievous toddler or older child.

❝A monitor that is designed to check for breathing and movement has a sensor pad that sets off an alarm.❞

 For up-do-date research done by the Foundation for the Study of Infant Deaths, go to www.sids.co.uk. Other products relating to combating cot death are covered on page 42.

Points to consider before buying: Baby monitors

Mains or battery operation A battery backup is useful if your home suffers from breaks in the power supply. This feature is also handy if you are visiting friends or family and rooms have no conveniently sited sockets.

Number of channels This allows you to select the best one for your location. A memory feature means you won't have to re-set this.

Range in a large house. If the signal must carry over fairly long distances and through thick walls, check its effectiveness as soon as you can and return it if it isn't up to the job.

Sound clarity is crucial. In certain conditions, some monitors suffer from annoying background static. If this is a problem for you, look for models with DECT (digitally enhanced cordless telecommunications), which have an interference-free digital signal.

Background noise in the room. If there is likely to be extra noise, such as passing traffic, or a cooling fan in the summer, it is helpful if the sensitivity of the child's unit can be adjusted.

Two-way communication allows you to speak to your baby and extends the value of the monitor as it can be handy when dealing with a toddler.

Remote control It can be very useful to be able to operate features such as the lullaby and night light.

Indicators for power on, system check, low battery and out of range can be very handy and reassuring.

Portable parent unit. Some can be clipped on to belts so that you can move from room to room without fuss.

Travel case if you travel a lot, a case to transport the unit is useful.

BABY CRYING ANALYSER

One interesting product on the market is the WhyCry monitor. This differs from other monitors in that it 'analyses' your baby's cries, the idea being that you have a better idea of what the cries mean (hungry, sleepy, in pain, and so on) and can deal with the situation accordingly.

You use a symptoms chart along with the monitor to help you analyse the cry. Arguably, this monitor may be an extra aid during the early weeks when you are lacking confidence, but you probably don't need one; parents tend to learn what their baby's cries mean naturally just by being attentive.

41

PRODUCTS TO COMBAT COT DEATH

Although cot death is rare, most parents worry about it to some degree when they have a new baby. Manufacturers have tapped into such parental anxieties, and in recent years a range of anti-cot death products have come on to the market.

These range from sleeping-position aids, which are designed to ensure your baby sleeps in the recommended position (see pages 60 and 67) to breathing monitors (see page 40). Baby sleep bags are now widely used instead of bedding (see page 64) and as there are no blankets there is no danger that your baby's head will get covered. They are made in winter and summer weights and usually come complete with advice on the amount of clothing that the baby should wear in relation to the temperature of the room in which he or she is sleeping.

You don't need to buy specialist products to guard against cot death unless recommended to do so by your medical adviser because your baby is viewed as being at particular risk. It's true that some products can help put your mind at rest if you are a particularly anxious new parent, but you shouldn't view them as a necessity. The Foundation for the Study of Infant Deaths gives very clear advice on putting your baby to sleep and on the risk factors known to be linked to cot death (see pages 54–5).

❝ Manufacturers have tapped into parental anxieties relating to cot death, and a range of anti-cot death products are on the market. ❞

Furnishing the nursery

Deciding what goes in the nursery is one of the most pleasurable aspects of preparing for a baby, but it sets up many choices from the décor to the size and type of bed and bedding. Tempting as it is to set the whole thing up ahead of the birth, in reality it makes sense to just get the basic decorating and organising done and leave the main purchases for later.

2

Cots

A cot is one of the few essential items you need for your baby, although even so, you don't have to rush into buying one ready for your newborn. A Moses basket, carrycot or crib or cradle (see pages 52-5) may be more practical when your baby is tiny - they all have plus points that can make the early days easier for you. Cots are equally fine for new babies. It is all a matter of personal preference.

CHOOSING A COT

There are so many different styles of cots around that many parents find the process of buying a cot a bit confusing. It is one of the most significant purchases you will make for your baby, so you want to get it right first time. The main differences, however, are fairly straightforward. Bear in mind that cots are rarely sold with a mattress, so you will need to buy one separately (see pages 56–60).

❝ When choosing a cot, think of its size, whether or not you want a drop-down side and if you need an adjustable base. ❞

Sizing up

Cot sizes vary. Cots designed to fit 'standard-sized' mattresses are a few centimetres narrower than cots designed for 'continental-sized' mattresses, although they are often a similar length. Cots will vary in size within these categories too. Cot beds, which are cots that convert into child-size beds, will be larger and need special cot-bed-sized mattresses. Look at a few cots before you buy to see if a larger size would be better for you – the measurements should be clearly displayed on the cot label.

The obvious advantage of a larger cot is that your baby will have more room – this may be more significant later on if the cot is used as a place to relax, looking at picture books or playing with toys. If your baby and you are happy to

 Large nursery chain stores, such as Babies 'R' Us, Mamas & Papas and Mothercare, will be able to advise you further. See pages 186-95 for Where to shop and also pages 204-11 for contact information for other retailers.

continue to use a cot until he or she is well into the toddling years, a larger cot may also be more practical. However, small cots are perfectly adequate for a growing baby and, indeed, they may be a better choice if space in your home is cramped. They also tend to be cheaper.

Fixed- or drop-sides?

Most cots available have drop-sides. One side of the cot will have a mechanism that is designed to let you lower the side so you can lift your baby in and out with ease, particularly when you have the base positioned at the lowest level (see right). Some cots have drop-mechanisms on both sides, so as long as the cot is not next to a wall you can choose which side to use.

How useful a drop-side is depends largely on the efficiency of the mechanism. Some designs work a lot more smoothly than others. 'Nudge and lift' mechanisms, when you push the side of the cot into a position where it can be lowered, can be useful because you can operate them with one hand. Other cots will have a trigger mechanism, a foot pedal or a couple of catches to undo.

Drop-sides can certainly be useful early on, but try out a few different types in the shops before you buy, and choose the one that seems easiest for you to use. Many parents find the whole process fiddly and prefer to lift their baby in and out without dropping the cot side, but if you have back problems, you may find drop-sides useful.

Solid ends or rails all around?

Some parents prefer a cot with rails all the way around because it's easier to see your baby if you just want to peek into the room (depending on where the cot is positioned, of course). The cot may also seem more open and airy to your baby. Solid ends, however, do give a cot a sturdier, solid look and your baby may prefer the more enclosed feel.

Height-adjustable base

The base height of most cots can be adjusted as your baby grows. A height-adjustable feature is especially useful if you are using a cot as opposed to a crib or Moses basket from birth. You can have the cot base on its highest level for the first few months, so you can lift your baby in and out of it easily.

Then, when your baby starts to move around more and pull him- or herself up, you can reposition the base at the lower level so that he or she stays secure in the cot. Cots tend to have a two- or three-position base, although a few have more. Two positions are fine for most people's needs.

❝Solid ends make a cot look more sturdy, whereas rails all round give it a feeling of airiness.❞

Teething rail

You won't know in the early days if your baby is going to be a cot-gnawer. However, chomping on the edge of a cot is a habit many babies do seem to relish. The teeth marks will certainly make your cot look less than new within a few months, but they shouldn't make it unusable. A teething rail is a protective covering lining the top rails of the cot. Choose a cot with one of these if you would rather avoid the risk of damage.

Castors

Some cots have castors, which can be a useful feature for moving the cot from your room to the baby's room, or to a different position in the nursery, as smoothly as possible. It also makes for easier cleaning under and around the cot. Ensure the castors are lockable.

The big sleep

The Foundation for the Study of Infant Deaths suggests that your baby sleeps in your room until he or she is six months old.

ALTERNATIVE TYPES OF COT

Other styles and designs are widely available, which, as well as looking a bit different, may have features that suit your needs better.

Cot beds

A cot bed is a cot with removable sides and end panel so that it can be converted into a toddler-sized bed when needed. These are increasingly popular and seem a logical way of lengthening the life of a cot as well as helping to make the move from a cot to a bed as smooth as possible for your child. Cot beds are larger than cots but are not necessarily much more expensive. You will need to buy a cot-bed-sized mattress rather than one designed for a cot.

Cot beds can be a practical option that suits many parents and children. However, you do need to think carefully about your future needs before buying one. The main disadvantage arises if you have a second child soon after having your first, when you will need the cot again just when you have converted it into a bed and your first child is growing attached to it. Buying a new bed, banishing your toddler from the cot bed and rebuilding it into a cot as well as dealing with another new baby may be something you'd really rather avoid.

Another possible disadvantage with cot beds is that as cots they often have fixed- rather than drop-sides (see page 45). You might also consider that as

❝ If there are castors on your baby's cot, ensure that they are lockable or they could pose a safety threat. ❞

Designer cots

At the pricier end of the market are 'designer' cots, shaped to provide you and your child with advantages conventional cots do not have – at a price. The main variation is in shape, for example, a corner-fitting cot frees up nursery space, while other cots come with a kit enabling their conversion into a junior bed or other furniture. Such products are pricey, and you'll need to consider carefully whether a hefty outlay is worthwhile.

Bedside cots

You can buy cots with a removable side so that you can position the cot right next to your bed and there is no barrier between you and your baby. These cots have a base that you can adjust to a wide range of different heights, so that your and your baby's mattresses can be lined up. This makes night-time feeding easier. If you find it harder to relax with the baby so close, the cot can be easily converted into a conventional cot.

❝ Cot beds are larger than cots but need not be more expensive. ❞

you will have to buy your child a 'grown-up' bed at some point, why not do it when he or she moves out of the cot? Cot beds are designed for children up to age six or so, but bear in mind the possibility that your status-conscious three- or four-year-old might start resenting having a baby bed when his or her friends have got 'proper' beds.

There are hammocks available for both babies and slightly older children. These are not suitable for children under one year old because:

- It will be very difficult to position the baby feet to foot.
- The baby can become overheated if the hammock 'wraps around' his or her body.
- There could be a risk of suffocation if the child's face is up against the fabric and the airflow is low.
- Babies should sleep on a firm horizontal surface so that the head isn't falling down towards the child's chest thus reducing the air intake.

 For more consumer advice about cots, go to the Which? website at www.which.co.uk.

SECOND-HAND COTS

Cots can be quite an expensive outlay, so many parents may be tempted to buy one second-hand or accept a hand-me-down from friends or relatives. If you do go for a used cot, it is important to consider the following advice:

- **Avoid old family heirlooms** (unless you are satisfied from a safety point of view – see the following points). The beautifully made cot you had when you were a baby may not meet current safety standards. These demand, for example, that cot bars are closely spaced and that paint must be both lead-free and have reduced levels of other potentially harmful chemicals. Continuing with a family heirloom may compromise your child's safety.
- **Measure the bar spacing** and the distance between the top of the mattress and the top of the cot. The bar spacing needs to be between 2.5cm and 6.5cm (1in and 2^1/$_2$in) and there must be at least 51cm (20in) between the top of the mattress and the top of the cot.
- **Check that the drop-side mechanism** (see page 45) works smoothly and stays reliably in the 'up' position, and that it would not be easy for a child in the cot to operate it

- If there is any sign of peeling paint, you should strip and re-paint the cot (see page 76).
- **Remove any transfers** on the inside of the cot because they could come off and become a choking hazard.
- **Check that there are no footholds** or cut-outs or ledges in the sides or the ends that could help a baby climb out.
- **Check that there are no protrusions** on the top rails of the cot where your child could catch his or her clothing or anything around his or her neck.
- **Check the mattress carefully.** You need to be sure that it is the correct size for the cot and that it is clean and has maintained its shape (see page 60). Check for tears or splits in the cover. Unless you know the history of the mattress and are happy with its fit and condition, it is sensible to buy a new one (see also page 60).

❝ If you buy a second-hand cot, it is important to check the points described on this page. ❞

For further information on buying second-hand products, see pages 197–9. If you are going on holiday, you may want to consider hiring some equipment: see page 200.

> If you are offered a cot for your baby to use when staying with grandparents or other hosts (some get stored in lofts for years ready to be produced for the next generation), check it as carefully as if you were buying it – see the box, below right. Buying or borrowing a modern travel cot may offer peace of mind.

" Travel cots usually fold and unfold using a central locking system that fixes the sides into place. "

Second-hand travel cots

Because travel cots may be used only occasionally it is tempting to buy second-hand. This is fine, but bear the following advice in mind:

- Ask for the original instructions if there is nothing printed on the cot.
- Check for obvious damage, such as holes in the mesh sides.
- Check that the mattress is in good condition. It may be hard to get a new one the right size and it is very important that you don't use a mattress that isn't a proper fit (see page 59). Furthermore, travel cots don't all have the same basic dimensions and the way the mattress folds is integral to the packing-away process – so one that is the wrong size can make it difficult to store neatly.
- Check the base for damage and also the frame for flaking paint and sharp edges.
- Try folding and unfolding the cot several times to check that it locks securely into place every time.

TRAVEL COTS

Travel cots are portable cots that you can fold up and put in a bag to take away with you. Most have a plastic or metal frame, woven fabric-and-mesh sides, and a hard segmented bottom with a folding, lightly padded mattress. They generally fold and unfold using a central locking system: you pull up a ring or handle in the centre of the base, click the sides into place, then push the handle back down to keep the locked sides rigid. A few models fold flat – these don't come with a bag and may not fold compactly enough to fit into a car boot, so are less suitable for travel (although they are fine as an extra cot for guest babies).

Some travel cot models can double up as playpens (see pages 177–8), although they won't provide as much space as conventional models. Some come with a bassinet for newborns, but generally they are not designed for very young babies as they do not have drop-down sides or adjustable mattress heights. A soft carrycot or Moses basket (see pages 52–4) can be just as portable but more suitable for newborns, and you can also buy lightweight fold-up travel carrycots from a range of baby catalogues.

Many parents get a lot of use out of travel cots. They can give you the freedom of staying almost wherever you want without having to worry about where the baby will sleep. A travel cot can also provide an extra sleeping place for babies who come to stay at your home. The playpen-sized models have even more potential for regular use.

However, countless travel cots are only ever used a handful of times. They can take up a fair amount of storage space even when folded, and even though they are portable they can be heavy to lug around, so you really don't want to buy one unless you are sure you'll get some decent use out of it. In other words, you only really need one if you will be making regular overnight trips to cot-free homes. Even then, if your baby is likely to stay somewhere overnight on a regular basis (say, with grandparents), it is worth considering buying a cheap standard cot instead to keep at their house. If you plan to stay at a hotel or holiday home, many

 Whether you use a cot from birth or transfer your baby to a cot after a couple of months, you will need to make up the bottom part of the cot with sheets and blankets folded under the mattress so that your baby sleeps in the 'feet-to-foot' position (see box on page 60) unless you are using a sleep bag. Place your cot out of reach of any cords that operate curtains as they could become wound around the child's neck.

will provide a cot or at least will be able to arrange hiring one for you. If you have a network of friends with young children, borrowing a travel cot for occasional use shouldn't be too hard.

❝Travel cots give you greater freedom as you don't have to worry about where your baby will sleep that night.❞

Points to consider before buying: Travel cots

If you decide a travel cot would be useful for you, bear the following points in mind when choosing one:

Some cots have wheels or castors. For reasons of safety, stopping the cot being moved inadvertently, there should be either four wheels, two of which should be lockable, or two wheels and two legs. This is a useful extra feature if you are likely to need to move the cot around. Wheels on the storage bag – either separate from those on the cot or poking from the cot through the bag – can be valuable as travel cots are often heavy to carry.

Weight and size are important. Some travel cots are more spacious than others. Look at the measurements – you may want to choose a larger size if you plan to use the cot as a playpen. Cot weights can vary a lot too. You'll probably appreciate a lighter one if you plan to travel by public transport or plane, rather than by car; however, these are also likely to be smaller. The weight should be labelled on the cot's instructions or specifications, but it may not be.

Folding mechanisms can be fiddly, although practice is often all that is needed. Try unfolding, folding and lifting a few cots in the shop before you buy. If this isn't possible, ask whether you can return the cot if you're not happy with the folding mechanism once you have practised at home.

If you want the cot to double as a playpen, then four rather than two mesh sides will give you and your baby a better view.

Some models have a range of extra features, such as a changing mat that fits over the top of the cot and toy storage pockets. Think about whether you will use these – you may be paying extra unnecessarily.

Look for a removable frame cover and mattress cover, for easy washing.

Clear, permanent instructions printed on the base of the cot are more useful than an instruction leaflet that you can easily lose.

MOSES BASKETS

These are designed to provide your baby with a safe and snug sleeping place for the early weeks; one which you can take elsewhere with ease. Many parents find the sight of their tiny newborn in a full-sized cot a bit disconcerting and are happier with the tighter fit of a Moses basket. It is also argued that new babies feel more secure and sleep better in the enclosed space that these provide.

Usually made from natural palm leaf, Moses baskets are light and have carry handles so you can move your sleeping baby if necessary. It is best to avoid carrying your baby around in the basket if possible, particularly if the handles do not meet in the middle. The basket also provides no protection for your baby if you slip or trip on the stairs.

You can place the Moses basket on the floor or, if you want your baby to be at a convenient height next to your bed, you can buy a fold-away stand to place the basket on. Check that this has a safety catch to prevent accidental closing. A PVC-covered foam mattress will normally be included with the basket, and often a canopy or hood, lining, quilt and fancy 'skirt' (the Moses basket equivalent of a valance). For the pros and cons of a Moses basket, see opposite.

" Moses baskets are light and have carry handles so you can move your sleeping baby if necessary. They can be placed on the floor or on a stand by your bed. "

If you want to further research Moses baskets and other sleeping products, turn to pages 204-11 for addresses and website details of many retail outlets.

The pros and cons of Moses baskets

Pros

- A light and portable sleeping place for your new baby
- When placed on a stand or other secure surface next to your bed, it enables you to reach your baby with ease for night-time feeds
- Snug-fitting sides can help make some babies feel more secure
- Fairly cheap choice if you have not yet decided what kind of cot you want and don't want to rush into anything
- Provides a familiar sleeping place for your baby if you are staying overnight away from home

Cons

- Some babies can find a cot hard to get used to after the confined space of a Moses basket – one of the reasons why many parents prefer to have their baby in a cot from birth
- An extra expense that is avoidable if you use a cot from the outset
- More expensive versions may look attractive but remember that your baby will be in the basket for a relatively short time (a couple of months or less is not uncommon)
- If you have other children, consider that a determined toddler or clumsy older child could knock over the basket on its stand
- Handles may be unsuitable for carrying the basket with your baby inside and may wear over time

Second-hand Moses baskets and cribs

Pre-cot sleeping units such as Moses baskets and cribs are sensible second-hand purchases. If you can borrow one or accept one as a hand-me-down, even better. They have many advantages for small babies but as you won't be needing one for long it could be worth saving your money to spend on a better-quality cot and mattress, which you will be using for longer.

If you do use a second-hand model, however, you need to be extra-careful about safety. On cribs, check that the locking pins are the correct ones for the model and fit neatly; on Moses baskets, check that the handles are in good condition. For both, check that the mattress has been kept clean and has maintained its shape – otherwise buy a new one.

CARRYCOTS

A carrycot is a sturdier alternative to a Moses basket although they share most of the benefits and disadvantages. If you have a carrycot option on your pushchair, you could use this as your baby's main sleeping place for the early weeks, although you may need to buy a mattress suitable for night-time sleeping (see pages 56–60). The clear disadvantage with this option is if you need to take your baby for a stroll and you want him or her to lie in the carrycot – unless you have the whole buggy contraption in your bedroom at night-time, you will spend a lot of time removing the carrycot from, and refitting it to, the base. You can buy separate carrycots, although they are not as widely available as Moses baskets. Choose one that is fairly lightweight as you may need to move your baby in it while he or she is sleeping. If your baby is to sleep outdoors at any time, you may need to fit a cat or insect net (see page 67).

CRIBS AND CRADLES

Some parents like the traditional option of a crib or cradle for the early months. These often have a gentle swinging or gliding action which helps to soothe some (but not all!) babies to sleep. They can also be locked into a fixed position for when your baby has settled. Avoid cribs or cradles that can't be stabilised like this, as you may find that the swinging motion doesn't suit your baby. Check whether the basic price of the crib or cradle includes a mattress (it varies). You can buy extras, such as crib bumpers and drapes that provide a canopy over the head of the crib. As with Moses baskets and carrycots, cribs are generally suitable from birth to around three to four months or when your baby starts to pull him- or herself upright.

SHARING YOUR BED

Some parents don't use a cot, crib or Moses basket at all, preferring to have their baby sleep in bed with them. Although this

The pros and cons of carrycots

Pros	Cons
• As part of a pushchair, the multi-purpose nature of the carrycot attachment (as a night-time as well as a daytime bed) is well liked by many parents • Generally more robust than Moses baskets so could be a useful investment for subsequent babies	• Depending on the model, they can be quite heavy and therefore somewhat cumbersome to move • Some are quite fiddly to remove and attach to a pushchair chassis

The pros and cons of cribs and cradles

Pros	Cons
• Swinging action can help calm many babies • Larger than Moses baskets so your baby has more room but can still feel snug • For the same reason, can be more suitable for bigger babies and can make the transition to a cot less disruptive • Convenient size and height for positioning next to your bed	• Cribs and cradles are not portable • Some babies hate the swinging action and you won't find this out until it is too late; even though it is gentle, the swinging motion can simply roll a tiny baby back and forth, and this can be irritating and uncomfortable • More expensive than Moses baskets – consider that your baby will be out of the crib before too long • As with other cot alternatives, cribs are an extra expense that is avoidable if you use a cot from the outset

can be comforting for you and your baby, a major research study has shown a link between cot death and bed sharing with babies under eight weeks old. The advice from the Foundation for the Study of Infant Deaths is that you should put your baby back in his or her own bed after you have cuddled or fed him or her if any of the following risk factors apply to you:

• Your baby is under eight weeks old.
• You or your partner smoke.
• You have recently consumed alcohol or taken drugs.
• You are extremely tired.

If you plan to sleep with your baby, don't let his or her head get covered by the pillow, use lightweight blankets rather than a duvet and make sure you place your baby so that he or she cannot fall out of bed.

❝A major study has shown a link between cot death and bed sharing with babies under eight weeks old. It is safer to put your baby back in his or her own bed after a cuddle or feed.❞

Mattresses

Cots don't normally come with a mattress, so you will have to buy one separately. You might think that choosing a baby's mattress would be straightforward, but high-tech innovations have burst on to the baby-mattress market and the traditional choice between spring interior or simple foam has become more complicated.

Your baby needs a mattress that provides good support but is soft enough to be comfortable and is the right size for the cot. What may make a difference to parents, however, are factors such as how easy the mattress is to keep clean and how long it will be needed for. Mattresses that are completely covered with PVC or another wipe-clean surface are the most practical and hygienic. Aesthetics can come into the equation, too – some mattresses look better than others. Many parents like the idea of a baby mattress that looks and feels like a mini-version of a traditional adult-sized mattress – for example, with springs and a quilted or 'ticking'-style covering – rather than a plastic-covered rectangle of foam.

> **66 As well as being comfortable and the right size for the cot, a mattress needs to be easy to clean. Choose from foam, spring interior or coir mattresses. 99**

TYPES OF MATTRESS

The two main types of mattress available are those with a foam core and those with a spring interior. You can also buy 'coir' mattresses, the core of which are made from natural coconut-shell fibres. Whatever you choose, the basic mattress core will be topped with one or more layers of other material – for instance, a waterproof covering and cotton padding. For the pros and cons of each type, see opposite.

Foam mattresses

Foam mattresses tend to be the least expensive. The simplest versions are made from a single layer of supportive foam completely covered with a wipe-clean, waterproof PVC cover. This cover protects your baby from dust mites (see box on page 58) as well as making the mattress easy to clean.

Some foam mattresses will be partially encased with PVC and have a section of ventilation holes, covered with fine mesh, positioned where your baby lies. These are designed to help your baby stay cool and to keep moisture – perspiration or dribble, for example – away from your baby (although they are not necessary and you shouldn't worry if your baby seems to lie everywhere other than over the holes).

More complex and expensive foam mattresses will have the same or similar foam core with a waterproof cover, but also a removable panel on top made from 'breathable' fabric which, again, is designed to draw moisture away and help prevent your baby from getting clammy and too hot.

The main advantage with these is that they are easy to keep clean because you can remove this section to wash it. There is no point in buying an expensive 'breathable' mattress if you're going to cover it with a PVC sheet to protect it.

Spring-interior mattresses

These traditional mattresses have a coiled spring interior with layers of (usually) felt and foam padding. They often have a

The pros and cons of mattresses
Foam mattresses

Pros	Cons
• Generally easy to keep clean • Good value for money • Can provide good support and resistance to denting	• Some parents may not like the idea of the basic PVC-covered mattress because of concerns about clamminess • Mattresses with ventilation holes can be more effort to keep clean if your baby is a dribbler or is often sick, because residue can gather in the holes and mesh

Spring-interior mattresses

Pros	Cons
• Many parents like the familiarity of a traditional spring mattress • The wipe-clean side is the recommended surface for your baby to sleep on because of the practical advantages, but you have the option of flipping it over onto the cotton side if you prefer – for example, if it is hot and your baby feels clammy	• More expensive than foam • The cotton side may be preferred for comfort but can be more difficult to keep clean (unless you buy a mattress with a removable panel)

cotton cover on one side and PVC or other wipe-clean material on the other. The cotton cover can be sponged or vacuum cleaned. As with foam mattresses, you can also pay a bit extra for a spring mattress with a removable top panel, which will have moisture-reducing elements.

Coir mattresses

These have a core of coconut fibre with other layers of different materials. The fibres are coated in latex for strength and protection and the natural fibre filling helps air to circulate through the mattress. These mattresses are available with a wipe-clean covering.

The pros and cons of coir mattresses

Pros	Cons
• One of the firmest types of mattress	• Less widely available than foam or
• Tend to be longer lasting because they hold their shape well, so could be a sensible purchase if you want to use it for more than one child or if you are buying a cot bed that will be in use for some time by one child	spring interior
	• Can be more expensive than the alternatives

Dust mites

Dust mites are microscopic organisms found by the million in every home. One of their favourite habitats is the warmth and humidity of a mattress. It isn't so much the dust mites themselves that create a problem, it's their droppings. When these minuscule droppings are inhaled, they can cause allergic reactions such as asthma and eczema in susceptible people.

Babies up to the age of two are especially sensitive to developing allergies, particularly if there is a history of this in the family. Owing to parental concern about this possibility, combined with a rise in the number of children suffering from allergies, anti-dust-mite baby bedding has become increasingly popular as a means of trying to reduce the risk of allergies developing. Dust mites are killed at a temperature of 60°C, so one option is to choose a mattress with a top layer that is washable at this temperature. Alternatively, go for one with a wipe-clean, waterproof surface.

Points to consider before buying: Mattresses

Mattresses come in two basic sizes, to fit the equivalent sizes of cot generally available in the shops. The size of cot the mattress will fit should be marked on the mattress and the cot. If the mattress is the wrong size, your baby could be dangerously trapped in gaps between the cot and the mattress. As a rule, the gap between the mattress and the cot should be no more than 4cm (1^1/$_2$in). If, however, you buy a cot that is smaller or larger than the norm, you can get mattresses specially made to fit your cot.

Many parents accept that some mattress staining is inevitable with a baby or small child, but you will want to keep the mattress as hygienic and clean as possible. A PVC-covered mattress or one with a removable top panel that you can wash at a reasonably high temperature is the most practical choice.

Squeeze a selection of mattresses in the shop if you can, and choose one that feels firm rather than soft. To compare firmness, squeeze at the edges and at the centre. Your baby needs a mattress that provides good support and won't sag, rather than a mattress he or she can sink into.

Look for a cot mattress that is 8–10cm (3^1/$_4$–4in) thick. Anything thinner won't provide the support your baby needs. Thin foam in particular can lose its shape and dent easily.

Foam mattresses are lighter than other types and are therefore the easiest to lift when changing bedding. This can be an advantage if your movement is restricted, for example.

If your family is prone to allergies such as asthma, a mattress that provides protection from dust mites (see box, opposite) would be a sensible choice. Manufacturers and retailers who sell mattresses with anti-dust-mite properties will usually advertise the fact loudly.

‘‘ Buying the right size of mattress is important as if it is too small for the cot, your baby could become dangerously trapped in gaps between the mattress and cot. ’’

USING THE MATTRESS FOR SUBSEQUENT CHILDREN

Retailers and manufacturers generally recommend that you buy a new mattress for each child. Cynics might say that this is because they want to sell as many mattresses as possible – but it is also true that a mattress can dip and sag with the weight of a growing baby and therefore might not provide an ideal sleeping surface for your next baby. A used mattress can also harbour dust mites, and babies who might be prone to allergies such as asthma may benefit from a new mattress if your existing one doesn't have anti-dust-mite protection.

The Foundation for the Study of Infant Deaths states that ideally you should have a new mattress for a new baby but if you choose not to, you can use the one you have as long as it was made with a completely waterproof cover (e.g. PVC) with no tears, cracks or holes, and is clean.

If you do want the mattress for more than one child, then paying a bit extra for a better-quality one that you can also keep clean easily will be worth your while. It is also sensible to take care of the mattress by turning it regularly to maintain its shape. If you don't know the history of the mattress – for example, if someone has given it to you – check it carefully for sagging. (For more advice on second-hand goods, see pages 197–9.)

'Feet-to-foot' position

Cot death is very rare. Since new recommendations on how babies should be put to bed were introduced some years ago, incidents of cot death have declined substantially. The key thing to remember is that babies should always be put to sleep on their backs with their feet near the bottom end of the cot so that they can't shuffle down under the covers. Place the covers no higher than the chest and tuck any surplus bedding under the mattress. Your midwife or health visitor will show you how to tuck your baby in like this.

❝Ideally, you should have a new mattress for a new baby, but you can use an existing one as long as it has a waterproof cover with no tears, cracks or holes, and is clean.❞

Bedding

Larger baby stores and catalogues will have a good selection of baby bedding for you to choose from. From simple sheets and blankets to baby sleeping bags, quilts for toddlers, cot bumpers and mattress protectors, the options are many and varied.

As with many other baby accessories, you don't actually need all that much. In terms of basic bedding, it makes sense to have a minimum of three bottom sheets, three top sheets and three blankets (all cellular, or one fleece and a couple of cellular – see page 63). Then you should always have one of each clean and ready if needed (if you'll be using baby sleep bags, you'll only need the bottom sheets). Buy the basic amount to start with, perhaps with a couple of spares, and see how you get on. You can buy small sheets and blankets for Moses baskets, prams, carrycots and cribs as well as larger sheets for cots and cot beds.

Parents of babies who are sick a lot may want to have more changes of bedding at hand.

SHEETS

These are usually sold in packs of two and you can buy them fitted or flat. Expect to pay less for crib or pram sheets and more for cot-bed sheets.

Fitted

These are very useful, especially as your baby gets older and moves around in the cot more. A fitted sheet won't ruffle and come away from the mattress as a result of a squirming baby. The main disadvantage with fitted sheets is that if the mattress you have bought is quite stiff and heavy, fitting the sheets may be cumbersome (although you'll soon get well-practised). Lighter, foam-based mattresses tend to be easier to fit sheets on to. Fitted sheets tend to be made of cotton jersey or terry (fine towelling cotton/polyester mix). Both have an advantage in that they don't need to be ironed (although ironing cot sheets, whatever they are made from, is probably not a priority for most busy parents!).

See the useful addresses section on pages 204-11 for retailers specialising in equipment for babies and toddlers. Internet shopping can be an especially good way to shop in the early days of parenthood.

You can cut up full-sized sheets to make smaller sheets for cots and other baby sleeping units. Just make sure edges aren't frayed, as little fingers can get caught up in the threads (you could just turn over the edges and whiz along with the sewing machine).

Flat

These tend to be used as a top sheet in combination with a blanket, although they are fine for use as a bottom sheet too. Generally they are more awkward to put on as a bottom sheet than fitted sheets, although many people prefer them. Flat

sheets tend to be made either from flannelette or plain cotton. Plain cotton has the advantage that it can be washed at higher temperatures, although it doesn't feel as soft as flannelette.

TEMPERATURE GUIDE

Small babies cannot regulate their body temperature very well so it is important not to let the room get too hot or too cold. Don't put your baby to sleep next to a radiator or heater or near a sunny window on a hot day. A comfortable room temperature for a baby is around 18°C.

If you feel uneasy about temperature, nursery thermometers are widely available. They are not expensive but are not a necessity either – trusting your instincts is probably just as good. Get into the habit of feeling your baby's tummy to make sure he or she isn't too hot or cold, and check for perspiration.

The amount of bedding you use should vary according to the season and temperature of the room. If you are worried about using too much or too little bedding and want to use a nursery thermometer to gauge this, use the following temperature guide:

❝ Vary the amount of bedding you use for your baby according to the season and temperature of the room. ❞

24°C: sheet only
21°C: sheet plus one layer of blanket
18°C: sheet plus two layers of blanket
15°C: sheet plus three layers of blanket

(Note that a folded blanket counts as two layers of blanket.)

Cot sheet fasteners

These are clips that fasten onto the bottom sheet under the mattress, keeping the sheet taut and preventing it from ruffling up. The fasteners allow you to use any small sheet as a cot sheet.

> **!** The advice from the Foundation for the Study of Infant Deaths (FSID) is that cot duvets, quilts and pillows should not be used until your baby is one year old. This is because they carry an increased risk of suffocation and overheating in younger babies. However, the use of sleep bags is recommended by FSID (see sleep bags, overleaf).

BLANKETS

The types of blankets most commonly available are cotton cellular, acrylic cellular and fleece.

Cotton cellular

These are 100-per-cent cotton. Their cellular structure (they are loosely woven such that they have small holes throughout – note that this design is not meant to reduce the risk of suffocation) means that they are warm in winter and cool in summer, so they are good for year-round use. They are also lightweight. They have the advantage of being washable at higher temperatures than fleece or acrylic.

Acrylic cellular

These are extra-lightweight and quick drying, with the same year-round usefulness as the cotton cellular type. They are generally similar in price to cotton cellular blankets, although they tend not to be as soft on the skin as cotton or fleece.

Fleece

Made from 100-per-cent polyester, fleece blankets are soft and easy to wash and dry. You can buy brightly coloured designs that often have attractive appliqué motifs. Fleece blankets tend to be more expensive than other types.

❝ Don't use cot duvets, quilts or pillows until your baby is one year old. Until then, use sheets and cellular or fleece blankets. ❞

See page 182 for information about bedding to protect the mattress from bedwetting once your child reaches toilet-training age.

OTHER BEDDING AND COT ACCESSORIES

Visit any nursery shop and you'll know that buying the bed provides numerous shopping opportunities for things to put in it apart from your baby! See opposite for the pros and cons of each of the following accessories.

Sleep bags

These sleeping bags designed for babies and young children have become increasingly popular in the UK as they have been for a long time in continental Europe. They usually have a full-length front zip or poppers at the shoulders and sometimes a zip at the side with sleeveless arm-holes. Rather than tucking your baby up at night under sheets and blankets, you simply zip or popper him or her into the bag. The bags normally come in either baby- or toddler-size. They are usually quite lightweight with minimal padding.

If the bag has a tog rating, choose low – anything higher than 2.5 togs could be too warm for your baby. Likewise, avoid bags with a hood or with full-length sleeves as these could cause over-heating.

The pros and cons of sleep bags

Pros	Cons
• No covers to throw off, so your baby stays warm all night	• Older babies and toddlers may find the bags constricting because they can't move around the cot as freely as if they had conventional bedding
• Takes away some of the worry about how many sheets or blankets you should be using (although you still need to be aware that your baby shouldn't get too hot – if the room is very warm, your baby may need a light sheet rather than the sleep bag) and you won't need to get anxious about your baby's head being covered with bedding	• Standing babies and toddlers may shuffle along upright in their bag, get entangled and fall on to the sides of the cot
	• Sleep bags can get grubby simply because you are unlikely to have changes at hand in the same way that you would have clean bedding - buy two if you can
• Something familiar to your baby that you can take away with you if you are staying elsewhere	• May be harder to modify for slight variations in temperature
	• Some retailers recommend that you avoid using these for smaller newborns (under 3.5kg (7lb 12oz)) who can be 'swamped' by them, so it is best to wait for a few weeks if you have a small baby

The pros and cons of other bedding and cot accessories

Quilts, duvets and pillows

Pros	Cons
• Getting used to a quilt in the cot may help with the eventual move to a quilt-covered bed • Easy to make up – no more fussing with blankets and top sheets	• Your baby may have grown attached to his or her blankets and may not like the idea of a quilt • An unnecessary expense – he or she will be moving to a bed soon enough so you could easily keep the 'baby bedding' going until then

Coverlets and comforters

Pros	Cons
• Less bedding to deal with at night-time • Usually part of a coordinated nursery range, allowing you to match your baby's cot bedding with the curtains, if you wish	• Tend to be more expensive than a sheet and blanket • You will probably need sheets and blankets anyway (as spares or for cold nights, for example), so it might be worth just keeping to these

Quilts, duvets and pillows

Once your baby reaches one year of age (see the box on page 63), it is fine to replace his or her baby blankets and top sheets with a cot quilt or duvet. You can get simple, understated designs as well as bright-and-breezy 'all singing, all dancing' quilts with built-in features, such as animal ears that squeak or crinkle when you press them. Pillows can also be safely used from the age of one year, but don't feel that you have to buy one – your baby will be used to sleeping without one and may even not want it in the cot.

Coverlets and comforters

A coverlet or comforter is a lightweight baby version of a quilt that can safely be used for babies under one year old because it does not have the soft padding of a standard quilt (although if your new baby is under 3.5kg (7lb 12oz), some retailers recommend you wait until he or she is this weight before you use one). It is as warm as a sheet and blanket combined.

❝ A pillow can be safely used once your baby is one year old, but he or she may prefer not to have one. ❞

65

Baby sheepskin fleeces

These are basically mini sheepskin rugs. They are designed to be soft and comforting for babies to lie on, and many parents who have used them feel that they calm and soothe newborns. If you buy one, make sure it is specifically for baby use.

Cot bumpers

These are soft pads that are tied to the sides of the cot, designed to give babies some protection from the hard sides. Bumpers are often sold as part of a bedding range so can be appealing to parents who want a matching nursery. However, they definitely come into the 'optional accessory' category.

The pros and cons of other bedding and cot accessories

Baby sheepskin fleeces

Pros	Cons
• Cool in the summer and warm in the winter • Many babies do seem to like the feel of them	• Not recommended for use as a sleeping surface for babies who roll over on to their fronts because of the risk of the soft fur surface restricting breathing • There is a possibility that they can harbour dust mites (more so than normal blankets), so you should wash them regularly in hot water, particularly if your baby is prone to allergies

Cot bumpers

Pros	Cons
• If you have a wriggly baby, bumpers do help prevent any little bumps in the night against the cot frame • They help stop dummies from falling through the gaps in the cot bars so are a useful way of keeping anything your baby is particularly attached to within reach • Some have touchy-feely materials or playthings attached so have the potential to provide a degree of in-cot entertainment	• The lifespan of bumpers can be limited – putting your baby in the feet-to-foot position to go to sleep means they are redundant in the early days, and once he or she gets more mobile and starts pulling up, bumpers have to be removed from the cot in case they are used as a lever to climb out

Cat nets

A cat net is a strong mesh net that can be fitted over a cot and helps to protect your baby against cats climbing into it. You can also get cat nets for prams (see page 152).

Insect net

This may be useful during the summer. It is a fine mesh net that fits completely over a pram, pushchair or carrycot and keeps bugs away from your baby's delicate skin, offering him or her protection from mosquitoes, flies, wasps and other insects.

SLEEPING POSITION AIDS

Anxiety about cot death, and the recommendation that babies should sleep on their backs with their feet at the foot of the cot, have led to a number of cot products coming on to the market that are designed to alleviate parents' anxieties about sleeping positions.

Cot bumpers need to be securely tied to the cot with the attached ties and these ties should be short to avoid your baby becoming tangled or chewing on them. These days any bumper you buy from a reputable shop is likely to have short ties, but check hand-me-down or second-hand bumpers: if the ties seem long – say, over 20cm (8in) per tie – trim them, making sure there are no frayed edges.

However, they are an unnecessary extra. It is not hard to tuck your baby in at the 'feet-to-foot' position once you know how to do it and, for babies who tend to roll naturally on to their fronts to sleep, the advice from the Foundation for the Study of Infant Deaths is that as long as you place them on their back each night and turn them during your normal checks, there is no need to be anxious.

The pros and cons of sleeping position aids

Pros	Cons
• Can provide some peace of mind for parents who are particularly anxious about their baby's sleeping position	• Any sleeping aid that your baby could use to lever him- or herself up with must be removed as soon as your baby is capable of pulling up – so you need to be vigilant • Remembering to position the sleeping aid in the cot each night in addition to washing, feeding, changing, tucking in and settling down is an extra night-time procedure you could do without

Changing tables

A baby changing table (sometimes called a baby changing unit or dresser) is a piece of equipment enabling you to change your baby's nappies at a comfortable waist-height rather than kneeling and bending over to change him or her on the floor. They either have an integral padded changing surface or you have to place a separate changing mat on top.

Changing tables come with storage units or shelves underneath so you can keep nappies, wipes and any other paraphernalia you may use all in one place, a handy distance from where you are changing your baby. Many have a plastic baby bath as part of the unit so that you can bathe your baby at a comfortable waist-height too. The changing surface covers the bath when not in use. Some also have accessory trays at hand-height, alongside the changing surface, so you can keep smaller bits and bobs, such as cotton wool or nappy creams, close at hand.

TYPES OF CHANGING TABLE

There are two main types of table: 'furniture'-style and open-shelf style. Both are widely available from a range of outlets. See opposite for the pros and cons of each type.

Furniture-style units

At the more expensive end of the market, these tend to be made up of a cupboard and drawers housed in a wooden waist-height unit and topped with a wide changing surface. You place a changing mat on top of this surface. The idea is that these units look like stylish pieces of furniture that you can use for storage beyond the nappy-changing months. Some units are big enough to use them to store your baby's clothes as well as changing materials.

Open-shelf-style units

These units usually have two wide shelves or storage containers, with a further changing shelf on top. Some are functional-looking 'trolley'-style units with castors so you can move the unit around if you want. Many of these include a plastic bath incorporated into the unit and have an integral changing mat. Others are made of wood and may have longer-lasting appeal because the shelves can be used for toys or books later on.

You will have a convenient waist-height surface upon which to bathe your baby in the early days, but placing a plastic baby bath (see pages 32–5) on any other stable surface or putting it in the bath itself is probably a more practical option for most people.

The pros and cons of changing tables

Furniture-style units

Pros	Cons
• You can carry on using these for clothes or toy storage even when your baby is well past the nappy stage – so although they can be quite expensive you can get use out of them for years to come • They often come as part of a set of nursery furniture so, if you want a coordinated look for the nursery, you can get a cot, wardrobe and shelves to match	• They can be pricey. In terms of what they are basically designed for – namely as a piece of equipment to help you change your baby with minimum fuss – a more basic unit will do the job just as well for a fraction of the price • Some can be quite bulky so are not suitable if space is at a premium • Think about whether you really want the piece of equipment you change your baby on to stay in your child's room for years to come – by the time your baby is a toddler or older, you may want to change the look of the nursery and might find other items of furniture that suit you better

Open-shelf-style units

Pros	Cons
• These are far cheaper than the furniture-style units • Tend to take up less space – if you are short on space, the less bulky the changing table, the better • Open shelving can be more practical because you can easily see and reach for nappies, wipes, etc., rather than having to search around in cupboards and drawers	• Many designs don't have the same 'staying power' as furniture-style units, because they aren't as multi-functional, and you are less likely to want to use one for general storage later on • Units that come with a baby bath can seem like a good idea, but because you have to fill and empty the bath by hand it can be a bit messy (and there's a fair chance of making a mess en route from the bathroom!) • Open shelving is not such a good idea once your child gets to the crawling stage

69

Points to consider before buying: Changing tables

Do you really need one? A changing table is a luxury item. Changing your baby on a wipe-clean mat on the floor is straightforward and practical, and the equipment for this only costs a few pounds (see pages 21-2). You can move the mat around the house, so you can change your baby at the most convenient place for you, or you could have two mats - one in the baby's room and one in the living room - so you don't have to move anything. Changing tables tend to tie you down to changing your baby in one place. If your changing table is in the baby's room, trudging there each time your baby needs a fresh nappy can become a trek you can well do without.

Portable units on lockable castors provide a bit more mobility, but in reality even these will probably end up 'parked' in the same place. Bear in mind that you may not use the changing surface part of the table for very long anyway - once your baby can move around, you may feel safer abandoning using the table altogether because of the danger of his or her falling off (see box, opposite).

That said, many people do find changing tables very useful. If you have a bad back and prefer to avoid crouching on the floor, a changing table can be a lifesaver because you are changing your child at a height that suits you. They can also help you keep all your baby's essentials in one place: you won't be searching around for a packet of wipes or the nappy cream because (if you are using the table as it is meant to be used) everything will be stored there.

If there is an incorporated changing mat, check that the sides of the mat are reasonably ridged. Anything that can help keep your baby secure is a bonus - just in case he or she does a flip when you are not concentrating.

Units with hand-height accessory trays as well as storage space underneath the changing surface are the most useful.

Think about whether you want your unit to be used for general storage later on, in which case it is worth considering one of the more expensive furniture-style units, or whether you are happy to have it as a temporary nursery item.

 Large nursery chain stores, such as Babies 'R' Us, Mamas & Papas and Mothercare, will be able to advise you further. See pages 186-95 for Where to shop and also pages 204-11 for contact information for other retailers.

OTHER TYPES OF CHANGING TABLE

There are a couple of other types of product worth considering.

Cot-top changers

This is a useful 'halfway house' between a changing unit and a simple changing mat. It is a rigid plastic rectangle with a padded changing mat that you place widthways on top of the cot at changing time. It means you can change the baby at a comfortable height but save on the space that an ordinary changing unit takes up. These are also far cheaper than standard changing units.

Fold-away changers

This style of changer is often seen in the toilets or baby-changing rooms of restaurants and shops. Generally made from plastic and having the appearance of a curved, tray-like shelf, the changer needs to be firmly fixed to the wall because it has no underneath support. When not in use, you fold it up on to the wall. This is especially useful if you are short of space, but cheaper options are available and because these changers don't have storage space, you can't keep your bits and pieces at hand.

 As with placing your baby on any high surface, there is an increased risk of accidents with changing tables. You should never leave your baby unattended on a changing table, at all times keeping him or her within arm's reach. Even small babies can move in ways you wouldn't expect and can fall off. If you have to answer the phone or door while your baby is on the table, make sure you take him or her with you.

❝ A changing table can be useful if you have a bad back, which prevents you from getting down to floor level. It also doubles up as a good storage container. ❞

Nursery lighting

You can buy lights specially designed for use in your baby's bedroom, which emit a soft light. Although an ordinary lamp or ceiling light is perfectly adequate for use in the nursery, many parents and babies like the soothing effect of a soft nightlight or lights that shine projected images, such as clouds or nursery characters, on to the wall and ceiling.

TYPES OF LIGHTS

As well as possibly helping your baby to go to sleep, a soft light can be useful for tending to him or her in the middle of the night. Some types can also be handy later on if your child dislikes the dark, as many do. You can choose from a range of different types of nursery lights. Those you are most likely to come across are the following.

" A soft light is useful for tending to your baby in the middle of the night. It can also be handy later on if your child dislikes the dark . "

Cot lights

These are attached to the cot and emit a battery-powered soft light. Many are sound-sensitive and light up when your baby cries, or you can switch them to be on all night. The more elaborate versions also play lullabies or 'nature sounds' as well as providing light. At the top end of the market are cot lights that project rotating images around the ceiling to the tune of lullabies.

Plug-in nightlights

These are small, round or oval lights that you plug directly into the wall socket. Some have light sensors so they come on automatically at night and go off during daylight.

 Electricity is an important safety issue when you have small children around. See particularly 'socket covers' on page 157 and 'curly flex' on page 159.

Light-effect bedside lights

You can buy bedside lights that project rotating images round the room, or ones that automatically fade out over a 15-minute period so that you have a brighter light to start with while you are settling your baby down.

'Instant' lights

These are battery-powered, cord-free, flat, rounded lights that you can fix on to the wall or place on any convenient surface. You push them down to activate them.

Although not designed specifically for use in a baby's or child's room, dimmer switches are also a very effective way of lighting the nursery. If you have one, there should be no need to leave on a nightlight as well, unless you want the automatic on–off element that some of these provide.

Some models of baby monitor (see pages 36–41) also come with a nightlight. If you decide to buy a plug-in nightlight, bear in mind that an innocuous-looking light rather than one with a children's character printed on it is probably the best choice if you want to reduce the chances of a curious child playing around with the socket.

Of course, some children are happier sleeping in a darkened room. You can buy blackout fabric for lining the curtains, which may be necessary, particularly if the bedroom window is close to a street light.

❝ Dimmer switches are a flexible way of lighting your child's room - the lights can be brightened or dimmed at the turn of a button. ❞

Other nursery accessories

When you first start choosing items for your new baby, you will be entering a world full of products you are unlikely to have even heard of during your pre-baby days, and you will need an explanation of what they are for before you buy. This is particularly the case with fixtures and fittings for the nursery.

The items in the jargon buster below may appeal to some parents – although, as many of them are sold as part of a coordinated nursery range (see opposite), they may well be chosen for their appearance rather than their usefulness. Fashions and tastes in nursery styles change along with product ranges.

" Decorating the nursery is high on the list of most new parents. "

Feeding time

Bear in mind that when feeding your baby you need to be thinking of your own comforts just as much as those of your baby. It is worth devoting some of your energy to arranging matters such as ensuring you have a comfortable chair for feeding – you could have this in the nursery or your bedroom for night-time feeds if you are not comfortable feeding in bed.

Jargon buster

Cot drape A light curtain that hangs above the head of the cot on a drape rod and is designed to give a romantic, old-fashioned look to the nursery

Cot tidy A flat, fabric holdall that fastens on to the side of the cot and which has open pockets for small toys and books

Cot valance Fancy frills to cover the cot mattress

Nappy stacker A hanging holdall, usually made from cotton/polyester with 'stacked' open pockets designed to keep a large pile of nappies neatly stored and easy to reach

Nursing chair A chair with low, padded arm rests and a gliding/rocking motion designed to provide a comfortable place for feeding and soothing your baby. On some models you can position the chair in a variety of reclining positions

COORDINATED FURNISHINGS

Most parents want their new baby's room to look attractive and newly decorated – this is, understandably, all part of the nesting process. Manufacturers and retailers tap into this instinct and produce ready-matched nursery ranges, so you can buy the wallpaper to match the curtains that go with the cot bumper and the lampshade, and so on. Catalogues from retailers are packed with photographs of rooms 'dressed' from head to toe in the latest nursery ranges. These can look very tempting, but when you stop to think about how much extra the 'bought-in' coordinated look can cost, the attractiveness may wane. It is true that most people are unlikely to get everything from one range and will pick and choose the items they most want or like.

However, in the quest for the perfect nursery, coordinated ranges do tend to encourage you to buy items you don't really need, and it can be tempting to think along the lines of, 'Mmm, that matching cot tidy could be useful and it's only another £15.' Do this a few times and the costs mount up.

There are bound to be 'extras' that you don't really need but that may prove useful or may simply be attractive to you. The point is that even picking and choosing a selection of these items can help to push the cost of furnishing the nursery right up. Remember, too, that you are also likely to be buying extra items for the early weeks when your baby will be sleeping in your room – a Moses basket with a stand and bedding, for example.

Looking ahead

Apart from the cost, there is another good argument for keeping the room décor and furnishings fairly simple. Although it is hard to imagine it when your baby is small, before too long he or she could be developing strong tastes in how his or her room should look, and this may well not include the Winnie-the-Pooh fixtures and fittings you decorated the room with before the birth. If you want to avoid the pressure to redecorate the room in three years' time, it is worth steering clear of character furnishings. No matter how cute they look now, they may just spell 'baby' to a pre-schooler desperate to be big. Likewise, think carefully before buying child-sized wardrobes and chests of

❝ It is hard to imagine when your baby is small, but before too long he or she will develop strong tastes as to how his or her room should look. ❞

drawers. As your baby grows into a toddler, space for toys and all the other paraphernalia that seem to mount up when you have children will be at a premium, so the more storage space you have, the better.

Painting the nursery

If you want to give the nursery walls a new look, keeping them plain is the most sensible option. It will be easier to match other items in the room to them if you want a coordinated look, and you can also decorate them with pictures, stencils or friezes. If you have access to the internet, you can get some interesting nursery decorating ideas from DIY retailers' and baby product websites.

Choose vinyl wallpapers or a water-based vinyl silk or eggshell paint. Water-based paints contain fewer solvents than oil-based paints, although they aren't particularly easy to clean. If you are going to paint the nursery, do it well before your baby moves in, so he or she isn't exposed to any fumes.

All standard paints are now lead-free, but you should be careful if you are placing an old, painted item of furniture in the nursery – the old paint may have a high lead content which, if it is peeling or flaking, could find its way into your baby's mouth at some point. You should be able to buy a test kit for detecting lead-based paint from your local builders' merchant.

Feeding equipment

What a baby drinks and eats can easily become a parent's obsession. From the first gulps from the breast or bottle to the refusals later on to eat anything green, worrying that he or she is having too little or too much is a parental emotion hard to avoid. Even if you are breast-feeding, there is still a range of accessories to consider. Once your baby goes on to solids, understanding food labels becomes an important skill.

3

Breast-feeding accessories

Breast-feeding is one of the most natural human functions so, arguably, there should be no need to kit yourself out with breast-feeding accessories – your breasts and your baby should do just fine together.

Manufacturers have other ideas, though, and have developed a wide range of breast-feeding products designed to help you out. To be fair, some can be quite handy. Whether or not they will be useful to you depends very much on factors such as how easy you find breast-feeding, how discreet you want to be when feeding your baby and what you want your baby to be fed on when you're at work or away.

> **❝ It can take a lot of practice to get used to a breast pump, but persevere and it may become a valuable part of your breast-feeding regime. ❞**

BREAST PUMPS

With a bit of practice you can express your own milk, so theoretically there should be no need to buy a breast pump. Having said that, some women find expressing their own milk difficult or they simply don't want to do it, and this is when you can find that having a breast pump is extremely useful. They enable you to express milk to give to your baby in a bottle or to store in the freezer for later.

It can take a lot of practice to get used to a breast pump. For some people it involves a lot of effort or inconvenience for very little gain, and if you give up altogether after numerous half-hours spent expressing little more than a mouthful of milk, no one can blame you. A breast pump that works very well for one person may not work nearly as well for the next. But if you find a pump that works for you, you may well find that it becomes an indispensable part of your breast-feeding regime.

 The website of the National Childbirth Trust is www.nct.org.uk, and for the La Leche League Great Britain go to www.laleche.org.uk.

If you can, try to borrow a couple of different types from friends so that you can have a few trial runs before you buy. Bear in mind that your milk supply may be variable; some days you can express more than on others, regardless of the type of pump.

There are three main types of breast pump to choose from:

Large electric pumps

These are the most effective. Used by hospitals, they are not widely available to buy but you may be able to hire one for a monthly fee from your local National Childbirth Trust (NCT) or La Leche League breast-feeding counsellor. If you will need to express daily at home – say, if you are going to work and need milk supplies ready for the next day – it is worth considering hiring one. The main disadvantage of these pumps is that they are quite bulky pieces of equipment and not at all portable, so they won't suit everyone.

Manual pumps

These are the simplest kind, worked by hand-operated pump action. They are light to carry around so are especially useful if you need to express while you are out or at work. They do, however, require a bit of a knack to operate effectively and your hand may get tired of pumping after a while.

Battery/mains-powered pumps

These are versatile because you can choose which power source to use. They

 If you choose a battery/mains-operated pump, use the mains as much as possible and, if necessary, take spare batteries with you if you are planning on expressing away from home. Losing pump power could be very inconvenient!

don't involve much effort, as you simply position the pump and switch on. They can be more expensive than the manual sort and are not as discreet as they make a slight noise when in use.

STORING YOUR MILK

Breast-milk freezer bags are widely available and are handy for storage. They have a measurement scale printed on them so you know how much milk they contain.

NURSING BRAS

A nursing bra helps you breast-feed with minimal fuss. They look much like ordinary bras but, depending on the style, are designed to let you drop, unzip or unclip the cups so that you can feed your baby without having to hitch up or prise open the whole bra. Nursing bras also tend to have wider straps, sides and back in order to provide you with adequate support.

Of the three types – drop-cup, zip-cup and front-opening – drop-cup are the most widely available. All require an element of practice to undo and do up without too much fiddling. Ideally you need to get the bra properly fitted before you decide which one to buy, as your breast size will have changed from your pre-pregnancy days.

Sleep bras are designed to support your breasts at night-time. These can also be useful for keeping breast pads (see right) in place while you are in bed.

" A nursing bra is specially designed so that you can feed your baby with minimal fuss. "

NURSING TOPS

Special breast-feeding tops are not essential but some women may find them useful, especially during the early days when they are getting used to breast-feeding and may want to do it as discreetly as possible. These tops normally have subtle 'flaps' and a zip or poppers across the front, which you lift up or undo and then put your baby to the breast. Your breast will be fairly well covered and your baby feeds through the opening in the top.

There is no need for special nursing nightwear – you just need something loose-fitting with fasteners at the front that you can undo easily.

BREAST PADS AND SHELLS

Breasts often leak during the early breast-feeding weeks, but you can protect your clothing by using breast pads. You put these inside your bra and they absorb the milk that leaks from your nipples. You can buy packs of disposable pads or ones that you wash and reuse. The reusable ones are better value for money in the long run but may be less convenient if you need to replace the pads regularly. Plastic-backed pads prevent your milk from leaking right through, although they should not be necessary unless ordinary pads don't provide you with enough protection. The plastic-backed sort can also encourage sore nipples unless changed regularly.

Breast shells have a slightly different purpose. Sometimes when you are breast-feeding, the breast your baby isn't feeding from can leak quite a lot. You can put a breast shell over this breast to gather the milk and store it for future bottle-feeding.

FEEDING PILLOWS

Many women find it more comfortable to breast- or bottle-feed with their baby resting on a pillow on their lap. You can buy specially shaped pillows that can make feeding even more comfortable (although any reasonably firm, standard bed pillow can work well). Alternatively, you can use the pillow to support your back while you are breast-feeding (or during pregnancy or labour).

Feeding pillows come in two basic styles – either 'V'-shaped or gently curved. Both styles can make feeding a more comfortable experience, although the 'V'-shaped style can also be useful as a back support on a chair (you may find these being marketed as all-round 'support' pillows rather than specifically as feeding pillows).

Many mothers swear by these pillows. The pillows normally have a foam, bean-bag or feather core (but you may not want to use one with feathers if you are worried about allergies). Bear in mind it may be worth buying a spare cover if available, as the pillows can easily become stained with milk.

BREAST PAIN RELIEF

There are times when your breasts can be very uncomfortable after you have given birth and during breast-feeding. Sore, cracked nipples are one temporary but unfortunate possible side-effect of breast-feeding. Soothing nipple creams, designed to help alleviate this, are available. Alternatively, midwives and health visitors often suggest gently rubbing expressed breast milk into the affected part.

Pain from engorged breasts – for example, when your milk first starts coming in or when you are producing more milk than your baby is taking – is very common. Vinyl breast packs are available that are filled with a gel and can be cooled in the fridge or warmed in a pan of hot water before being placed inside your bra. The best overall 'cure' for painful breasts and nipples, however, is to persist in trying to establish a comfortable breast-feeding routine.

❝ Breast pain can be extremely uncomfortable, so get advice from your midwife, health visitor or GP as soon as possible. ❞

Bottles and teats

A baby's bottle seems such a simple and uncomplicated item, yet getting the right bottle for their baby is a task many parents find troublesome. That's because different bottles – or more specifically, teats – suit different babies, and the one that your friend's baby happily uses won't necessarily be the one that yours will take to.

Many parents hit the jackpot first time, either because they are lucky or because their baby isn't fussy. For others, an experimental process will be necessary. This may be especially the case for mothers trying to wean their baby off the breast and on to the bottle.

" Different bottles and teats suit different babies, so be prepared to experiment for the best results. "

Number of bottles

If you will be bottle-feeding more or less from the birth, you'll need to buy six bottles. Even if you are breast-feeding or planning to, there is a good chance that you will buy bottles at some point during your baby's first year, so it's worth familiarising yourself with the advantages and disadvantages of different types of bottle, and perhaps having one or two to hand in case you need them.

TYPES OF BOTTLE

The basic choice of bottle is between standard and wide-necked. Within these two categories there are bottles with added features, such as an easy-to-hold shape or heat-sensitive material. Teats normally come with the bottle but you can also buy them separately. It pays to have more teats than bottles, as they will need replacing (for more on teats, see pages 85–6). The usual amount of milk a bottle will hold is 225ml (8fl oz), although you can get smaller bottles for new babies. See opposite for the pros and cons of each of the following types.

Standard bottles

These are the narrow, cylindrical bottles that are a familiar sight. You can buy them plain or decorated with various babyish designs. They will fit a range of standard teats and have self-seal lids.

Wide-necked bottles

These are shorter and fatter than standard bottles but take the same amount of milk. They usually take silicone rather than latex teats and will usually have a self-sealing lid.

Unusually shaped bottles

Some bottles are shaped to be easier for little hands to hold. Oval-shaped bottles with a hole in the middle for fingers to grip are widely available. You can also buy bottles with rounded ridges along the sides and 'nipped in' waists. Wide-necked, angle-shaped bottles, on the other hand, are designed to be anti-colic. Because the top of the bottle is at an angle, the milk always stays in the teat, so there's less likelihood of the baby swallowing air. The manufacturers say that this reduces colic.

The pros and cons of bottles

Standard bottles

Pros	Cons
• Most widely available • Most likely to fit accessories such as bottle coolers and sterilisers • Least expensive type of bottle	• The narrow neck means they can be trickier to fill than wide-necked versions, so are more likely to result in milk powder spills

Wide-necked bottles

Pros	Cons
• Easy to clean and fill • Some of these bottles are designed to have anti-colic properties, as babies are less likely to gulp down air with their milk (see above)	• Less versatile, in the sense that once you start using a wide-necked bottle you'll probably be sticking to bottles and accessories made by one or two manufacturers • Take up more space – for instance, you may not be able to fit as many bottles in a steriliser

Unusually shaped bottles

Pros	Cons
• Easy-grip bottles are useful for encouraging older babies to drink unaided • Angle-shaped bottles are worth a try if your baby has colic	• Some unusually shaped bottles can be more difficult to clean, as milk residue gathers in the nooks and crannies – you may need to buy a special bottle-brush • They may not fit in your steriliser • The main potential advantage of anti-colic bottles is fairly short-lived as colic is unusual after three months of age

The pros and cons of bottles

Heat-sensitive bottles

Pros	Cons
• May be useful if you are particularly anxious about giving your baby too-hot milk	• Arguably unnecessary – using the inside of your wrist to test milk temperature is a time-honoured method that works well enough for most people • You should always test the temperature anyway just in case the temperature sensor isn't working

Bottle 'sets' or 'systems'

Pros	Cons
• Versatile • Good value for money if you stick with the same bottle system	• Your baby may prefer a 'non-system' type of bottle or spout, in which case the bottle system isn't good value for money or versatile • You may be buying into the particular manufacturer's range of products so may be less willing to experiment with other brands

Disposable bottles

Pros	Cons
• Convenient to use when out or on holiday as there is no need for a steriliser	• Expensive if used daily • You may not feel comfortable with another disposable item – you'll be generating enough waste from other baby-related paraphernalia

Glass bottles

Pros	Cons
• Clean without staining • Environmentally friendly if the glass is recycled	• Breakable

Heat-sensitive bottles

A fairly recent innovation, heat-sensitive bottles have an in-built temperature sensor, which changes colour if the milk is too hot.

Bottle 'sets' or 'systems'

Some manufacturers produce bottle sets that include attachments, such as handles and trainer spouts, which you can fit on to the bottles when your baby reaches the appropriate stage. The idea of these systems is that you stick with the same bottles from birth to weaning and simply customise them for your baby's needs and capabilities.

Disposable bottles

These are not so much disposable bottles as disposable, sterilised bags that fit into a bottle. You put them into the bottle, fill them with milk, and throw them away when your baby has finished.

Glass bottles

You may be surprised to hear that you can buy glass feeding bottles. They are not widely available but parents who are concerned about chemicals in plastic bottles and about the environmental disadvantages of using plastics often opt to buy them.

TEATS

The type of teat you choose may make a difference to how well your baby feeds, so you might need to experiment with different types. Teats are made from either silicone or latex. Wide-necked bottles normally only take silicone teats while standard bottles can take either.

Traditional or orthodontic?

The usual shape for a teat is either the traditional bell shape or a bulbous, orthodontic shape that is meant to resemble more closely the shape of a nipple and the contours of your baby's mouth. Again, you may need to try both to find which type your baby prefers. Some teats have anti-colic valves, which are dents or holes in the teat that are designed to reduce the amount of air your baby takes in with the milk. Some also have 'dimples' on the teat, which are specially designed to mimic the feel of a real nipple.

❝ Some teats have anti-colic valves that are designed to reduce the amount of air your baby takes in with the milk. ❞

 With bottle-feeding comes sterilising - see pages 87-90 for information on the choices available to you. You might also want to consider buying a bottle-warmer, in which case see pages 91-3.

Flow rate

How fast the milk goes into your baby's mouth depends on the number and type of holes in the tip of the teat. You need to choose a teat with a 'flow rate' that suits your baby. Teats range from slow-flow through to medium- and fast-flow, for babies who can cope with more milk with each suck. You can also buy variable-flow teats, which suit babies of all ages as the flow is determined by how hard they suck.

BOTTLE ACCESSORIES

You will need a bottle-brush to clean your bottles properly before sterilising and a teat-brush to get into the tips of the teats. Optional extras include those that are listed in the jargon buster, right.

> " Teats range from slow-flow through to medium- and fast-flow, for babies who can cope with more milk with each suck. "

Jargon buster

Bottle cooler bags Insulated bags that keep milk fresh when you're out and about; single or multi-bottle sizes are available (if you have a changing bag, this may include a bottle-insulating compartment anyway)

Bottle-drying rack A unit for the draining board designed for easy drying of hand-washed bottles and teats

Dishwasher basket A small basket for keeping your teats, dummies, etc., in one place inside the dishwasher (otherwise they can fall through the gaps)

Portable bottle-warmers A piece of equipment that allows you to warm up a bottle easily when you are out and about

Go with the flow

The flow rate suitable for your baby is not necessarily related to his or her age - some new babies may prefer a medium- or fast-flow teat, as they can get tired if they have to suck hard to make the milk flow. You probably need to change the teat to a slower-flow one if your baby is spluttering his or her milk out and choking, or to a faster one if he or she is sucking hard but seems to be getting frustrated.

Sterilisers

All your new baby's feeding equipment (including breast pumps) must be properly sterilised. Milk is a breeding ground for harmful bacteria and small babies are especially vulnerable to them.

If equipment is not sterilised, the bacteria can multiply swiftly; regular sterilising makes sure the equipment is a 'no-go' area for bacteria. A steriliser is not essential – bottles can be sterilised in a pan of boiling water – but if you are planning to bottle-feed your baby, it can be a useful piece of equipment to have and will make your life easier.

If you are mainly breast-feeding but, say, giving your baby a bottle a day, a steriliser is an unnecessary extra. You can buy one later if you find you are making up more bottles than you expected or if you decide to switch to bottle-feeding completely.

❝A steriliser is not essential but if you are planning to bottle-feed your baby, it can be a useful piece of equipment.❞

TYPES OF STERILISER

Apart from the boiling-water method (see box on page 89) there are three methods of sterilising: steam method, cold-water method (also known as chemical sterilisation) and the microwave method. You can buy sterilisers designed specifically for each of these and the pros and cons for each are given overleaf.

Steam sterilisers

With this type, you place your bottles upside-down in the steriliser, add water and switch it on. The water is heated electrically. When sterilisation has finished (usually after about ten minutes) the steriliser switches off automatically.

Cold-water sterilisers

Here, tablets or liquid containing diluted bleach are placed into a measured amount of cold water inside the steriliser tank. Bottles must then be completely immersed in the solution, making sure there are no air bubbles where bacteria could survive (you need to be especially

See the useful addresses on pages 204-11 for contact information for a wide variety of retailers, both large and small.

The pros and cons of sterilisers

Steam sterilisers

Pros	Cons
<ul><li>Easy and quick to use</li><li>Minimum pre- and post-sterilisation preparation</li></ul>	<ul><li>Tend to be pricier than other types of steriliser</li><li>You need to be careful not to burn your hands once sterilisation is complete – the inside of the unit can be very hot</li></ul>

Cold-water sterilisers

Pros	Cons
<ul><li>Nothing to heat up so no chance of painful accidents</li><li>No need for electricity or a microwave so you can use it anywhere</li><li>Traditional method that many hospitals use – some parents find it reassuring to stick with the way it was done while they were in hospital</li></ul>	<ul><li>More fiddly than other methods</li><li>You need to keep track of when you last changed the solution – it needs to be changed every 24 hours</li><li>Relatively slow sterilising process</li><li>Heavy to move when filled</li></ul>

Microwave sterilisers

Pros	Cons
<ul><li>If you have a microwave, this is likely to be the most convenient method for you</li><li>Fast and simple</li><li>One of the cheapest methods</li></ul>	<ul><li>Generally these only take four bottles – other types take six or eight – so they are not as convenient for parents of exclusively bottle-fed new babies (or multiple births!)</li><li>Some sterilisers can't be used in the most powerful, modern microwaves – check before you buy</li><li>Some may not fit in smaller microwaves</li></ul>

careful about this if the bottles are sterilised lying on their side). Sterilisation usually takes around 30 minutes. The bottles need to be rinsed in recently boiled water before use to completely get rid of the chemical solution.

Microwave sterilisers

In this method, you place the bottles in the steriliser with a small amount of water, fasten the lid, place it in the microwave and operate according to the manufacturer's instructions. Sterilisation takes about ten minutes.

Heating your baby's milk in a microwave oven is quick and convenient, but even if the bottle feels cool, the milk can be unevenly heated. If you choose to use this method, select the shortest time possible, under-heating rather than over-heating, shake the bottle thoroughly and check the milk yourself before feeding the baby.

The boiling-water method

If your baby has just an occasional bottle and you don't want any more baby paraphernalia taking up space in your kitchen, boiling bottles in water is a cheap and relatively quick method of sterilisation. You put the items you want sterilised into a large pan of boiling water. The water should be brought back to the boil and boiled for ten minutes before removing the items. A disadvantage with this method, however, is that it can make rubber teats spongy and swollen – check them regularly and always discard any that seem damaged.

❝ If you have only the occasional use for a bottle, use the boiling-water method, as described to the left. ❞

Points to consider before buying: Sterilisers

You may want to buy a steriliser with additional features. These can include:

Steriliser bottles If you only need to sterilise one bottle at a time, instead of using a steriliser you can buy specially designed steriliser bottles for microwave sterilisation (you shouldn't try to sterilise normal bottles in the microwave without the right equipment as there could be unsterilised spots left). This is a quick and simple method, especially for parents of babies who are not exclusively bottle-fed.

Cold-water sterilisers can be very heavy to move when filled with water, so a sturdy handle is important.

Some sterilisers come with tongs and/or a tray to hold smaller items, such as teats, so you don't have to reach too far down into the unit to retrieve them.

Sterilisers that take both standard and wide-necked bottles are more versatile – you may find that your baby gets on better with one type of bottle, so if your steriliser only takes the 'wrong' type you could find yourself buying another.

Larger sterilisers that take up to eight bottles at a time can be more convenient if you are doing a lot of bottle-feeding.

Sterilisers that have space for feeding bowls and training cups will be useful during the weaning stage. Babies start using these items from four months or so and it is recommended that all feeding equipment should be sterilised at this age).

Some sterilisers can be used with more than one method of sterilisation – for example, microwave and cold water. This can be useful if you need to sterlise when away from home if a microwave may not be available.

Travel sterilisers are smaller than standard ones so can be handy for holidays. Generally they are designed to accommodate a couple of bottles rather than the six or so that standard sterilisers take. Some are suitable for just one method of sterilisation (for example steam); others can be used with more than one. Alternatively, as long as a microwave is available, steriliser bottles (see left) or reusable steriliser bags are easy to carry and simple to use.

Bottle-warmers

Using a bottle-warmer can be a convenient way of ensuring that your baby's milk is heated to the right temperature. You generally fill the warmer with water, which is then heated by an element, which in turn heats your baby's feed. Most will fit jars of baby food as well as various sizes of bottles.

The length of time the feed will take to heat varies depending on the warmer, but you can generally expect a 125ml (4fl oz) bottle of milk from the fridge to warm up in about six minutes. A larger amount of feed will take longer and feed already at room temperature will take a shorter time to heat.

" A bottle warmer takes about six minutes to heat an average-size bottle taken from the fridge. **"**

TYPES OF BOTTLE-WARMER

There are three main types of bottle-warmer: standard, 'feeding-system' and portable.

Standard bottle-warmers

These are the most common type, and will heat up one bottle of milk (or jar of feed). You place the bottle in the central vessel of the warmer, fill around it with water from a jug, and switch it on. An element heats the water, which, in turn, heats the bottle. These warmers normally have an indicator light that goes off when the milk reaches the right temperature, and a thermostat, which keeps the temperature of the water constant. Most will need de-scaling regularly unless you use softened water. It is useful to buy one with a timer so you know how long the milk has been in – not all warmers have these.

Parents' discussion sites on the internet can be a valuable source of information about looking after your baby and buying different products. Try www.motherandbabymagazine.com or ukparents.co.uk (see also page 195).

If you think you will be using the bottle-warmer to heat jars of food as well as milk, you should choose one that has an adaptor for holding jars at an easily reachable height – otherwise you can end up reaching down into the hot warmer for your jar. Some warmers have the facility to heat food in a bowl too.

❝ Some warmers have the facility to heat jars of food or food in a bowl as well as bottles of milk. ❞

'Feeding-system' bottle-warmers

These are more sophisticated than the standard type. They heat milk in the same way but also have a cooler section that keeps a couple of filled bottles chilled and ready for warming. This could be particularly useful at night if you want to avoid having to go to the kitchen to get the milk out of the fridge (although you could simply use a standard warmer and have the filled bottle ready in a cool-

bag by the bed). It's worth looking for one with added extras, such as a timer and jar holder.

Portable bottle-warmers

These are the simplest type of bottle-warmer available. They allow you to warm up a bottle easily when you are out and about, although the milk will generally take longer to warm up than in other types of warmer, so you have to plan ahead to some extent. They work in various ways, depending on the product. Car bottle-warmers can be plugged into your car's cigarette lighter and have a webbing strap or wrap that fits around the bottle of milk or jar of baby food. You need to plan ahead to use it otherwise you could have 15 minutes of hungry screaming.

Thermos produces a bottle-warmer that works like a flask. It is made up of two sections: an inner flask and a lid deep enough to hold a bottle. Before you go out, fill the flask with boiling water and attach the lid. When you need to heat up the bottle of milk, remove the lid, put the bottle in it and then fill around it with the hot water from the flask. The milk can take just a few minutes to heat up. The water should stay sufficiently hot for a few hours to warm the bottle.

DO YOU NEED ONE?

Whether or not you need a bottle-warmer depends on how happy you are with using the other standard bottle-warming methods. The time-honoured method of sticking the bottle in a jug of warm water for a couple of minutes has been used by generations of parents and is a cheap and effective way of heating milk that requires no extra equipment. Save time and effort for night feeds by keeping some water hot in a thermos flask. You will need to test the milk's temperature by shaking a few drops on to the inside of your wrist. If it's too hot, you just put it in a jug of cold water for a short time.

If you know that you will need to heat up a lot of bottles and you want to get it right first time, every time, then a bottle-warmer could be for you. A bottle-warmer may suit those parents who don't like the idea of microwave heating or the warm jug of water method. Bottle-warmers can be particularly handy for night-time feeding: as long as you get everything ready the night before, you can have the warmer next to your bed and you won't have to trudge to the kitchen to prepare the milk.

Don't automatically assume, however, that your baby will reject unheated milk. Babies don't have to have their milk warmed and some are perfectly happy with room-temperature or even cold milk. You could save yourself money and time by finding out sooner rather than later whether your baby is actually bothered about milk temperature.

"If you are heating bottles by standing them in hot water, always test the temperature of the milk before giving it to your baby. Sprinkle a few drops on to the inside of your wrist."

Baby food and drink

The official guidance is that a mother should try to exclusively breast-feed for the first six months so her baby receives all the nutrients he or she needs. However, when this isn't possible – either through choice, lifestyle or inability to breast-feed – infant formulas are available to ensure infants can still receive the correct nutrients they need.

Before the age of six months, babies' delicate digestive systems aren't fully developed enough to cope with any other food sources. However, many infants begin to show signs that milk isn't enough some time between four and six months and many parents are happy to start introducing non-milk foods, in a process called weaning. Simple signs to look for include: your baby starts to sit unaided; he or she shows an increased interest in other types of food; he or she appears to be hungry even after a feed, and your baby begins to put things into his or her mouth.

The weaning stage can be a daunting (and trying) time, but it is best to remember that there is no right or wrong way of weaning as all babies are different and will have different needs and tastes. Most parents start off by giving their babies baby rice, which you buy in packets and mix with boiled water or milk. Baby rice is very bland, so your baby gets used to the texture of food before experiencing any real taste. Smooth vegetable and fruit purée can also be used as first foods. Formula or breast milk should still be the main

source of nourishment. By the time your baby is about six months old, as long as everything is mashed up or puréed, his or her taste buds and stomach are more or less ready for most of the foods you eat.

SHOP-BOUGHT OR HOME-MADE?

The big question faced by most parents once they start proper weaning is whether to go for shop-bought packets and jars of food, to make home-made baby food, or to do a bit of both. Manufactured baby foods have clear advantages in terms of convenience. You don't have to do any scraping, boiling or puréeing – you just pop open the jar and down it goes (with some babies, without any need for heating up either). If you feed straight from the jar, you don't even have to do any washing-up.

For many parents, however, this kind of convenience isn't the be-all and end-all. Home-made food also has clear advantages, not least because you know where the food comes from and that it doesn't contain any unwanted ingredients. You can alter the texture of the food and experiment with different tastes and mixtures to suit your baby's progress (use either a special blender for baby food or a hand-held blender; or you can mash soft food with a fork).

Home-made meals can be cheaper if you're using the same foods that the rest of the family is eating, and can also help babies get used to the taste of home-prepared food. Neither does home-made food need to be much less convenient – you can, for example, make batches of food to freeze in freezing trays sold in nursery stores or just use ice-cube trays and defrost portions as you need them.

But whatever your intentions, it is fairly likely that you will buy at least some manufactured baby food, even if only to keep in the cupboard for an emergency or when travelling. So how do you choose between the large number of brands and types available?

TYPES OF BABY FOOD
Manufactured baby meals come in two main types: 'wet', pre-cooked meals, mostly found in jars and cans; and dry foods in packs (these have to be mixed with water or milk). Frozen types of baby

Infant formula milk

Formula milks have been developed to mimic the properties of breast milk. Like breast milk, these have the right balance of vitamins, minerals and fat for a growing baby. The only main difference between breast milk and infant formula is that breast milk also contains antibodies that help the baby's immune system. Most people buy their formula milk (often referred to as just 'formula') in powder form in large tubs, although you can also buy ready-mixed formula, which is useful for holidays or other times when mixing your own is inconvenient. Make sure you choose the type of formula suitable for your baby – it should be clear from the labelling on the tub (often by age), which is the most appropriate.

There are three basic categories of formula milk, regardless of the brand:

- Standard formula milk, suitable from birth or if changing from breast-feeding.
- Milk for 'hungrier' bottle-fed babies, also suitable from birth but curd- rather than whey-based so has a different balance of milk proteins, which some babies find more filling.
- 'Follow-on' milk, for older babies from around six months and toddlers – rich in iron and vitamins C and D, which are important for older babies and which cows' milk does not provide in adequate quantities.

The main type of formula milks are developed using cows' milk proteins. However, there are other types on the market. Hydrolysed protein formula and soya-based formula are available and often subscripted by a GP or a qualified health professional when an infant might have an allergy or intolerance to cows' milk.

Speak to your health professionals first if you think your baby is having problems digesting the formula you are using – very few infants aged under six months develop dairy intolerances.

> **Do not give infants younger than six months food containing:**
>
> - Gluten, found in pasta, bread, or chapattis made from wheat
> - Nuts and seeds, including peanut butter and other nut spreads
> - Eggs
> - Raw or cooked shellfish
> - Citrus fruit and juices
> - Honey
> - Soft and unpasteurised cheeses

Sweet talking

Government recommendations are that baby foods should usually be free from, or low in, sugars, including those from fruit juice. This is to reduce the risk of infants developing dental caries in their first teeth. Nevertheless, many of the baby foods available contain sugar, fruit juice or both.

Breakfast meals are likely to contain sugar, some 'savoury' meals contain glucose syrup, a form of sugar, and many desserts contain some form of added sugar. Sucrose, glucose, dextrose, glucose syrup, honey, fruit juice concentrates and fruit syrups are all types of sugar to look out for on the label. If one of these is listed in the first couple of ingredients this means it is high in sugar. As a general rule, if the sugar content under 2g or less is considered to be a low sugar content.

foods are also available. The meals are labelled or categorised depending on what age of baby they are aimed at. Within these you can choose between the increasingly popular organic ranges or non-organic types.

Whether organic is better than non-organic is under debate. There is currently no evidence to state that in terms of nutrient content one is better than the other. Organic foods use different farming and rearing methods to ensure they are not harmful to our environment. However, whether a parent chooses organic or not is a matter of personal choice.

Then you have a choice from a vast range of recipes – from turkey dinner and apple pie dessert to chicken korma and courgette risotto with banana.

LOOKING AT THE LABELS

Beyond making sure that the meal is the right one for your baby's age, it is well worth studying the ingredients on the jar or packet. What you see may well influence your choice. Remember that ingredients are listed in order of quantity, so the first is the major ingredient, the last the smallest.

Nutrients to look out for

Some ingredients in baby foods that can give cause for concern are additives, such as starches, gums and maltodextrin, which are used to thicken and alter the texture of food. Critics feel that because starches absorb water these can 'pad out' the meal so there's less 'real' food in it. Some brands clearly state that they don't add starches, while others contain more starch than the ingredients featured in the name of the product. Check the label for a lower starch content if you want more food for your money and more nutrient benefits.

Other ingredients with health implications are:

- **Gluten** can cause a reaction in some people. Babies under six months old should not be given wheat-based cereals because these contain this protein. Some food for babies under six months is not gluten-free. However, the presence of gluten as an ingredient has to be stated on the label.

- **Salty** food should not be eaten by babies. Although the amount of salt that manufacturers can add to baby food is regulated, you should still try to choose the lower-salt varieties. Watch how much salt you add to your home-made foods as well. Try to not add any extra salt to your baby's food and limit the intake of highly salty foods, such as bacon and sausages. Infants up to the age of one year should only consume 1g of salt per day.

- **Pesticide residues** can be present in many foods but the law requires that all baby food meets stricter limits on pesticides, and some pesticides will be banned from crops used in baby food.

Meaningless labels

Some manufacturers exploit the worries that many parents have about the foods they are giving their children by making claims on the label that, although true, have little or no useful meaning. Treat with a pinch of salt baby-food labels that make the following claims.

- 'No artificial flavourings': official recommendations are that baby foods are flavoured only with natural foods, or food extracts and oils.
- 'No artificial colours': these are banned in baby food anyway.
- 'No added salt': the amount of salt that can be added to baby food is controlled by law.
- 'No added sugar': this doesn't mean no added fruit juice.
- 'No preservatives': preservatives are not allowed in baby food (although some antioxidants, such as vitamin C, are added to stop food going off).

 Advice on safe and healthy eating is available from the Food Standards Agency (www.food.gov.uk) and the public services website www.direct.gov.uk.

COMPARING BRANDS

Different brands and ranges of baby food contain different proportions of ingredients and different levels of starch and sugar. Try to get into the practice of looking at the labels to see what kinds of ingredients baby meals contain. Top tips to remember are:

- **Look at the label,** noting manufacturing food claims, nutrition information and appropriateness of food type for your baby's age group.
- **Compare different manufacturer's products** – this may seem like extending the length of your shopping trip, but it will become quicker as you get to know your products.
- **Ingredients are listed in order of weight,** with the biggest first. Use this to choose products that are lower in salts and sugar content.
- **Review the quality of ingredients.** If the ingredient appears in the name of the food (for example, strawberry in strawberry yoghurt), the percentage must be stated, but for other ingredients the exact percentage does not have to be labelled – so it is this order that is the key to how much sugar and starch, for example, is in a product. Added sugars and fruit juices can encourage a sweet tooth, and water, as well as starch, may be used to 'pad out' a meal.

❝ Fruit juice contains naturally present sugar, so always water down the juice before giving it to your child. ❞

DRINKS

Milk and water are the best drinks for your baby or toddler. Milk suitability is as follows:

- **Whole milk** for infants above one year old.
- **Semi-skimmed milk** can be introduced from two years old.
- **Skimmed milk** isn't suitable until after five years old.

Sometimes it may not be very practical for parents to stick to this, particularly if you are outside of the house. Small children like fruit juice and it can provide them with important vitamins and minerals. Fruit juice does contain naturally present sugar, however, so it is advisable to water down the juice. It is also best to try not to use fruit juice as the main drink as it can be filling.

Some fruit drinks are marketed specifically for babies and are usually some sort of non-acidic fruit juice, such as apple, mixed with water. But it is important to remember, nevertheless, that even when diluted, it can still contribute towards tooth decay. Although products such as these may be handy for travelling, it is far cheaper to simply water down your own cartons of juice and give this to your baby in a cup (juice in bottles is not recommended as it can encourage tooth decay). Squashes, fizzy drinks, flavoured milk and juice drinks are not suitable for young babies; this includes diet or no-added-sugar varieties. It is good practice to try to limit the intake of these from a young age.

Highchairs

A highchair of one form or another is one of the few essentials for an older baby. They are not suitable for use until your baby can sit unsupported (usually at around six to nine months), although you can buy highchairs that are adaptable for young babies.

Before the six-month stage, many parents use a reclined cradle or other type of baby chair at feeding time (see pages 28–30). Once the time is right for a highchair, though, you and your baby will appreciate the benefits. You won't have to crouch down for feeding and he or she will feel part of the family sitting at table-height to eat meals.

As long as your baby is strapped in, a highchair will provide a safe eating place and a prime viewing position for him or her to watch people busying about the kitchen. You can also use the highchair as a play chair, by placing toys on the tray and letting your baby entertain him- or herself as you get on with other things. Some types of highchairs convert to chairs that toddlers and even older children can use.

TYPES OF HIGHCHAIR

There are many types of highchair available and all with different features and benefits, so it is well worth going in to the shop with a clear idea of what you need. See below and overleaf for the pros and cons of each of the following types.

❝A highchair provides a safe eating place and prime viewing position for your child.❞

Standard highchairs

These are the simplest type of traditional-looking highchair and have one height position. You can buy fold-up versions and models with useful extra features, such as a detachable tray.

The pros and cons of standard highchairs

Pros	Cons
• Generally the cheapest type, apart from travel highchairs (see page 104)	• Lack of seat-height adjustability means they're less versatile
• One height is adequate for most people	• Not all will have other useful features like an adjustable or detachable tray
• Tend to be lighter and fold flatter than other types	

Multi-position highchairs

With these you can adjust the seat height so that you feed your baby at a low or high level. Many have five or six adjustable height positions. On some models you can also adjust the seat so it reclines. Most can be folded and many have extras, such as varied-position trays.

Convertible highchairs

Often referred to as 'three-in-one' combinations, these can be used as a highchair for younger babies then converted into a toddler-sized chair and matching low table when your child reaches the self-feeding stage. They are usually made of wood. On some models the wooden seat has a padded cover, but if there isn't one built in, you should be able to buy one separately.

Baby-to-adult highchairs

Unusual-looking and innovatively designed, these can be adjusted for use by all ages. They have a long, slanting wooden back that is interspersed with slats or slots into which you position a wooden seat, footrest and safety bar. Where you position them depends on how big your child is. Your baby will normally sit, secured with a safety bar and a harness, at the table. When your child gets older, you can remove the safety bar and adjust the height of the seat. An adult would be able to use this as an occasional chair with the seat at a low position.

The pros and cons of multi-position highchairs

Pros	Cons
• Height adjustability means you can feed your baby at a position that suits you best – self-feeding toddlers may prefer the low level, for example, or you can use this level for a smaller baby if you prefer to feed him or her lower down	• The adjustments may not be particularly easy to make – many parents find one position they are happy with and stick with it, so the height-adjustment element may be a bit redundant
• Models with reclining seats can be used for newborn babies and to bottle-feed, so extend the lifespan of the highchair	• Some models can be quite heavy and cumbersome to move – also they are fairly large so aren't a good choice if you're short on space
• Depending on the model, they are not necessarily much more expensive than the standard type	

The pros and cons of highchairs

Convertible highchairs

Pros	Cons
• Toddlers who protest at being put into their highchair, whether in a high or low position, may feel more grown-up (and eat more happily) with their own chair and table	• Cube chairs can't be folded and so take up permanent space in your kitchen
• Style-wise, at least, the wood design can be more acceptable to many parents as a piece of kitchen furniture	• If you have your second child soon after your first, you're unlikely to get the best use out of the chair because you'll want to use it as a highchair again before your elder child has had full use of it as a chair and table
• Once you have finished using the chair and table in the kitchen, they can go into your child's bedroom as an extra piece of furniture (larger models can be used for children up to the age of five years)	• Less likely to have the 'added extras' of some other highchairs, such as recline positions and an easily removable tray
	• Some models are cumbersome to assemble – try before you buy if possible

Baby-to-adult highchairs

Pros	Cons
• A versatile seat that can 'grow' with your child	• More expensive than most other highchairs
• Designed so your child can always sit at the correct height at the table	• Can be heavy so not very manoeuvrable
• Fits in well with other modern-looking dining and kitchen furniture	• With a second child, you may find yourself buying a standard highchair anyway, as the idea is that your first child should still be using the seat
• No need to buy a booster seat or other children's chairs or tables when your child gets older	• Alternatively, you may decide to spend another £100 or so on another of the same seats, and so on with any subsequent children – and you could end up feeling that you have bought yourself a lifestyle rather than a highchair

Large nursery chain stores, such as Babies 'R' Us, Mamas & Papas and Mothercare, will be able to advise you further. See pages 186–95 for Where to shop and also pages 204–11 for contact information for other retailers.

Table-mounted chairs

These are portable chairs that can be used from the age of six months and are attached directly to a table. The usual design is a seat of washable fabric secured around a metal frame that you screw or clip to the table-top. The child should be secured with a safety harness and sits with his or her legs dangling underneath. When you first use one you may feel it is unsafe because your child's legs are not taking any of the weight, but the chairs are designed such that, as long as the table is stable, your child's weight is balanced and supported. Once you have finished with it, you unscrew the seat and fold it flat.

Folding booster seat

This is a sturdy plastic seat that you place on a conventional dining chair and attach with straps to the back and bottom of the chair, allowing the child to sit at the table with the family at meal times. These seats are only suitable for children who can sit up unaided. It is important that they are correctly attached to the dining chair so that the seat cannot slip either forwards or sideways and that the mounted seat is stable enough to cope with the inevitable wriggling. Some also have rubber pads on the seat base for extra security.

There are models with removable trays and most have adjustable seat heights. As with table-mounted chairs, keep sharp and hot items well out of the child's reach. Folding booster seats are also handy to take with you when visiting friends and grandparents.

It is important that table-mounted chairs are correctly attached otherwise there are serious safety concerns. They must never be used on a pedestal table, lightweight or glass-topped tables, where the top is not attached to the table legs or tables with a bevelled edge. There must also be no table cloth; the surface of the table must be clean and grease free, and hot or sharp items must be moved far away from the child's reach.

Fabric seat

These are designed primarily for temporary use and comprise a fabric part that is attached to a traditional dining chair and is worn by the child in a trouser-like arrangement. Designs vary – some have a 'hood'-style back that you slide over the top of the chair, others have a harness attached to a wide strap that you Velcro around the back of the chair, and another is a padded back-and-seat cushion with a standard harness. They are particularly useful when going out as they usually fold away into a fabric bag and are light and easy to carry. As with folding booster seats, the stability of the dining chair is important.

Baby sitter seat

This is a seat made from plastic that is moulded so that the baby's own body weight holds him or her in the seat. It is designed for young children from about four months to a year and can be useful when feeding young children. However, there is no safety harness to keep the child in place and the seat will almost certainly be used on an elevated surface – not the place to have a child who may wriggle out of the seat or manage to slide it across the surface and fall on to the floor.

The pros and cons of highchairs

Table-mounted chairs

Pros	Cons
• Not expensive • Handy for taking with you when travelling • Useful if you are very short of space	• Must be constantly checked to ensure they are firmly attached to the table • Can't be used on all types of table • Not suitable for a child to play with toys • Have to keep cutlery and hot drinks out of the child's reach

Folding booster seat

Pros	Cons
• Not expensive • Handy for taking with you when travelling • Useful for getting your toddler involved in family mealtimes • Easy to keep clean	• Dining chair plus booster seat must show no signs of tipping • Have to keep cutlery and hot drinks out of the child's reach • Not as compact as a table seat, and can be bulky and heavy

Fabric seat

Pros	Cons
• Cheap • Small and light to carry	• Not suitable for everyday use • Your child will not be at table height

Baby sitter seat

Pros	Cons
• Handy for feeding young children	• No safety harness • Child sits at an elevated height

Portable highchairs

Travel or portable highchairs are useful if you are likely to be visiting child-free relatives or friends on a regular basis, travelling to holiday homes or visiting cafés and restaurants that don't make provision for babies. There are various types available, ranging from table-top fabric chairs that attach to the table to fold-up booster seats and harness-style models (see pages 102–3). They are mostly lightweight and fold up easily – some types can even fit into a handbag.

As with ordinary highchairs, travel highchairs are only suitable for babies who can sit unaided.

Some parents use a portable highchair instead of a standard highchair in their own home. If you are short on space or money (they are a lot cheaper than most normal highchairs), or simply want to avoid any extra clutter, most travel highchairs are perfectly acceptable to use at home. You just need to make sure the model you want fits your particular type of table or chairs.

If you are planning to buy a travel highchair specifically for use on a holiday, bear in mind that lots of holiday homes and hotels will provide one anyway, so check this out first.

SECOND-HAND HIGHCHAIRS

Highchairs are often used second-hand. If you do buy a second-hand one or use a hand-me-down, check that:

- It is stable, sturdy and isn't missing any screws or bolts.
- It has an integral harness; if it hasn't, buy a separate harness and use it every time your baby is in the chair.
- There are no sharp edges or elements, such as cracks or breaks on the plastic tray, that could pinch your child.
- No foam is exposed on the seat – babies could very easily pick it out and choke on it.
- There is no flaking paint or splinters.
- Locks and catches to keep it open are working properly.

❝ Check that a second-hand highchair is stable and has a harness and catches that work properly. Also ensure there are no sharp edges. ❞

 For further information on buying second-hand products, see pages 197–9. If you are going on holiday, you may want to consider hiring some equipment: see page 200.

HIGHCHAIR ACCESSORIES

There are toys designed specifically to be used on a highchair (although bear in mind that your baby may get just as much entertainment from a wooden spoon and a plastic box). The main advantage with highchair toys is that you can attach them to the highchair, either with a suction pad or tied to the frame, so you won't be constantly stooping to pick up the toy once your baby has discovered the joys of throwing things on the floor.

The drawback is, of course, that he or she will get bored with seeing the same old highchair toy every day, so try to vary the toys if you want to get maximum benefit. You can find a range of toys suitable for highchairs at children's stores.

Another potentially useful accessory is a plastic mat that you can place under the highchair to catch all the spills. This is especially handy if you have a floor that is a nuisance to clean. Make sure the mat covers a reasonable area around the highchair, as spills won't necessarily be falling directly underneath. Mats are widely available from children's stores.

❝ Choose toys that can be attached to the highchair – an asset once your baby has discovered the joys of throwing things on the floor. ❞

!

- Never leave your baby unattended in a highchair.
- Secure your baby in the highchair at all times with a safety harness – either the integral one supplied or a separate one complying with British Standard 6684. Attach the harness as soon as your child is seated and make sure that your child has a leg each side of the crotch strap or bar.
- Be careful lifting your child in and out of the highchair (if your baby is struggling or catches his or her foot under the tray, the whole highchair could fall over).
- Do not use a highchair on a slippery, raised or uneven surface.
- Store the highchair out of your child's reach when folded.
- If you have to do something away from your baby, make sure the highchair is positioned away from anything your baby could reach.

105

There are numerous types of highchair on the market but, whichever sort you pick, you should look out for certain qualities before you make your choice.

Padding and comfort Your baby will be using the highchair a lot and anything that helps to make him or her want to stay in the chair rather than squirm out will be of benefit. Likewise, a larger seat is better than a smaller one.

Ease of cleaning A fabric cover that you can remove and put in the washing machine just isn't practical enough. You need to have a seat you can wipe after every meal.

Not all highchairs fold up, but if you want one that does, you should be able to fold and store it with minimal effort – otherwise it's bound to stay standing as a semi-permanent kitchen fixture. Models that stand when folded, rather than needing to be leaned against a wall, can be useful if the chair is to remain in the kitchen rather than be stored away (although these can take up more space). With some highchairs you have to remove the tray before you fold it – this is an added burden if you plan to put it away regularly.

The tray As a general rule, the bigger the tray, the better. Think of the tray as needing to be roomy enough to hold a selection of playthings rather than simply a bowl or a cup. Indentations in the tray, such as a dip for holding a cup, are a nuisance rather than a good design feature because they make cleaning more difficult. Likewise, angular ridges on the edge of the tray simply become food traps. A high, curved rim is best.

Can you detach the tray? A detachable tray is a useful feature if you would like the option of your baby sitting right up to the main table (although the design of some tables may not allow you to push the highchair close enough). It will also make cleaning easier. Check that the tray is simple to detach, however, otherwise you may not bother. Alternatively, a flip-over tray will also enable your baby to feed at the table.

Can you adjust the tray? Adjustable trays give your baby more room as he or she grows and can make it easier to get the child in and out. If you like the look of a highchair with a fixed tray, look at the gap between the tray and the chair and think about squeezing a chubby toddler in there – some chairs with fixed trays have quite a narrow gap. Others are positioned too far away for some babies to reach their food comfortably.

The harnessing system It should have a crotch restraint (strap or bar) to prevent the child slipping forwards out of the seat and an effective waist strap and shoulder straps to prevent the child standing up on the seat. Straps that can be removed for washing are an advantage.

Sharp edges Feel under the tray and around the edge of the seat area for sharp rims. You don't want to be scraping your toddler's thighs every time you lift him or her in or out of the chair.

The height/seat/tray-position adjustments Are these simple and quick to do? If not, you may well not bother using them. Try them out in the shop.

Bibs

By the time your baby reaches the weaning stage, you are already likely to be feeling that the cycle of clothes-washing is playing a rather dominant role in your life. Anything that helps to keep that pile of soiled and smelly baby garments to a minimum has to be a piece of equipment worth having.

The bib is a trusty stalwart of babyhood, which has saved many a garment from the wash cycle until absolutely necessary. Many parents with babies who are sick or dribble a lot are likely to have been using bibs regularly from the early days, but when the likes of puréed carrot and strawberry fromage frais start to appear on the scene, the true value of a decent bib is evident.

66 Anything that helps to keep that pile of soiled and smelly baby garments to a minimum has to be a piece of equipment worth having. 99

TYPES OF BIB

The traditional style is a semi-circle of towelling with ties for the neck, but you could also choose pull-on bibs, long-sleeved cover-all 'super' bibs, rigid plastic bibs with in-built 'crumb' trays, disposable bibs, and more. All will protect your baby's clothes and so do the job, but there are differences between the various types.

As long as the bib doesn't get in the way and isn't uncomfortable to wear, it's a case of the bigger, the better once your baby gets into the idea of feeding him- or herself. You don't have to buy bibs, however. A muslin cloth tied at the neck will cover your baby very well and washes easily. It's when your baby gets a bit older and more coordinated in terms of pulling off whatever you put on him or her that you may appreciate a manufactured bib with child-proof fastenings. See overleaf for the pros and cons of each of the following types.

If you enjoy online shopping - and it can be a real boon during the early months of parenthood - see pages 204-11 for mail-order and online shopping contacts. You can't have too many bibs and they are readily postable.

Traditional towelling bibs

You can buy small versions of these for young babies, to help protect clothes from milk spills or dribbling, or you can buy larger versions for when your baby starts to eat. You usually attach them with ties or a Velcro fastening, or they have a stretch head-hole that you pull over your baby's head.

Plastic scoop bibs

These have an in-built curved 'catch' tray at the base of the bib so food falls into the tray rather than into your baby's lap. They usually have an adjustable hole and popper neck fastenings. Some bibs have a towelling top and removable plastic scoop.

The pros and cons of bibs

Traditional towelling bibs

Pros	Cons
• Simple and inexpensive (often available in multi-packs) • Highly absorbent • Some have a waterproof plastic backing to prevent liquids from soaking through – a good choice if your baby is a dribbler • Easy to fold up and carry around with you when you go out	• Baby foods can easily stain them even if you wash them at high temperatures, so don't expect them to stay looking new for long (although brightly coloured ones may hide the stains better than pastel-coloured ones) • Waterproof-backed bibs cannot normally be washed at the same high temperatures as all-towelling versions • Some are too small for an older baby, especially when he or she starts to self-feed

Plastic scoop bibs

Pros	Cons
• Wipe-clean; some can also be put in the dishwasher • Good for babies trying to self-feed	• Rigid plastic versions can be stiff and uncomfortable around the neck – look for those with a soft neck rim or ones made from flexible rather than stiff plastic • Older babies may enjoy tipping everything out of the scoop tray • Larger scoop bibs may catch on the highchair tray and prove awkward to use

Cover-all bibs

Usually made from plastic-coated fabric or flexible PVC, these bibs are designed to provide maximum protection for toddlers in particular. As well as covering the front, some versions have full sleeves while others cover the shoulders and upper arms. They are generally fastened with ties or Velcro.

Disposable bibs

Throw-away bibs are usually made from strengthened paper. You normally buy them in packs of 20 and they will often have a waterproof backing as well as an absorbent front. Adhesive tapes attach the bib to the baby's clothes, although some brands have neck ties.

The pros and cons of bibs

Cover-all bibs

Pros	Cons
• Best for top-to-toe protection	• Some children dislike being 'dressed up' to eat and may protest
• Can be used as protection for painting and other messy activities as well as feeding	• Full-arm versions sometimes have uncomfortable elasticated wrists – check for potential discomfort before you buy
• Often have bright, fun designs that appeal to toddlers	• Depending on the brand, can be relatively expensive
• Easy to clean	

Disposable bibs

Pros	Cons
• Great for holidays when you don't want extra washing	• Can be expensive if you use them on a daily basis – although you don't have to use a new one every time
• Useful to keep as an 'emergency' bib in the car or changing bag or just to have on you when you're out and about	• Relatively easy for your baby to pull off, so ruining the whole point of the exercise
• Handy for wiping everything up once your baby has finished eating	

If you enjoy travelling with your baby, see the tips on pages 136–7, which are designed to help make life on the move as straightforward as possible.

Bowls, spoons and trainer cups

Although you can use bowls and small spoons that you already have in the house, those specifically designed for weaning have advantages.

BOWLS

Plastic bowls with high sides and a 'lip' or gripper on the edge for you to hold are convenient for when you are feeding your baby. It is useful to have a lip to grip hold of, not least because your baby is bound to try to swipe the bowl out of your hand at some stage. Once your baby is trying to self-feed, bowls with lower, gently curving sides and a textured easy-to-grip rim all round the edge can help him or her keep control.

'High-tech' versions of feeding bowls include those with a compartment in the base into which you put hot water to keep the food warm; heat-sensitive bowls, which change colour when the food is cool enough to eat; and bowls with a suction base, which helps prevent spillages. Some parents find these innovations useful although they are not a necessity and can make the process of feeding more complex than it needs to be. Bowls with fun designs on the base may seem gimmicky but some children like to get to the bottom of their food to reveal the picture, so they can be a useful feeding aid.

SPOONS

Standard teaspoons are often too deep for babies to get a decent mouthful from. Shallow spoons made from flexible plastic will help a young baby to feed and are also popular as a teething accessory with some babies. Self-feeding babies and toddlers will need a deeper spoon with an easy-to-grip handle. As with feeding bowls, you can buy 'high-tech' versions of spoons: for example, airplane-shaped spoons or, rather more usefully, spoons that change colour when food is too hot for a baby.

" Once your baby is trying to self-feed, bowls with lower sides and a textured rim can help him or her keep control. "

110

TRAINER CUPS

Moving from a bottle to a cup is one of those little developmental landmarks that parents often feel proud their baby has reached. You may already have a cup spout attachment for your baby's bottle if you use a 'feeding system' (see page 85). These spouts are soft and pliable and can be very useful for that first cup experience.

"When your baby is first starting to use a cup, a small one with a soft plastic spout is ideal."

Handles

Easily grippable handles are a big plus, especially when your baby is first starting to use a cup, because he or she will find it easy to control. The drawback is that handles also make it easier for your baby to wave the cup about – not a problem if you have a leak-proof cup (see below), but messy if you haven't. Many parents find that their babies are happy with smooth-sided beakers from an early age, and stick with these.

If you have a leak-proof beaker, check that the lid as well as the beaker are dishwasher-proof – some lids are not.

Spouts

When your baby is first starting to use a cup, a small cup with a soft plastic spout is ideal as a transition from a bottle to a cup. Once your baby has got used to the idea of a cup, there are various types you can try. The simplest are those with a basic lid and a spout. These are widely used, but don't expect this type of cup to keep leaks and spills completely at bay. As long as it is kept upright it will be fine, but once tipped sideways it may leak.

Many parents prefer the security of a leak-proof cup. These usually have a self-sealing valve so that the drink is sealed in after each sip. However, younger children may not get on with them, simply because they may have to suck quite hard to get the drink out. The valve can also wear out over time and you'll need to replace the lid. In addition, some of these cups have lids that are quite hard to get off for filling and washing. Despite these drawbacks, they are highly popular.

A compromise is a 'travelling' cup, with a spout that you can lift up when your child wants to drink and put down when he or she has finished. Your child can suck normally to get the drink out. The lids to these are often screw-on, so are easy to remove but don't come off when the cup is thrown on the floor. However, this sort of cup may not be completely leak-proof if it gets jiggled around a lot in your bag or in the car, as it is still possible for juice to leak through the spout when it is down.

Once your child can use a straw it isn't such a problem if you are out and about and have forgotten his or her cup – you can simply use a mini-carton of juice. However, a juice carton can be something of a liability: small children often squeeze the carton too hard and juice goes flying everywhere. An interesting product to prevent this is a juice box holder: you place the carton in it and your child holds this instead of the carton. Of course, you do have to remember to take the juice box out with you instead of the cup.

❝ A juice box holder is a useful addition to your travelling accessories as it helps prevent juice spillages when a carton is accidentally squeezed too tightly. ❞

Travelling with your baby

Once you have a baby, getting from A to B safely, comfortably and as easily as possible demands that you buy a certain amount of baby equipment specifically for travelling. Apart from the essential pushchair or pram (see pages 140-9), you have to buy a car seat if you have a car or if you will be getting lifts in one. This chapter includes guidance on the many baby travel accessories on offer.

4

Car seats

A car seat is one of the very few items you must buy for your baby if you will be travelling by car as it is illegal to carry a baby in your arms in a car. If your baby is going to be travelling in a car from day one – for example, from hospital to your home after the birth – you must buy a seat before the birth.

It is also the only piece of equipment you should definitely buy new. A car seat that has been in a crash may have sustained invisible structural damage that could affect its ability to protect your child adequately. In addition, older models will not meet the newer, stricter, safety requirements.

Car seats vary considerably in price, but you'll pay more for added extras, such as deeper padding, footrests, belt hooks to keep the belt out of the way while you are putting your child in, and additional comfort adjustments.

SEAT CLASSIFICATIONS

Child car seats are split into five different categories: 0, 0+, 1, 2 and 3. Weight, not age, is the critical factor in determining which seat is right for your child. Some seats span two or more groups (for example, some seats are suitable for children between 13 and 25kg (29lb and 3st 13lb), and so are in groups 1 and 2).

Car seat classifications

Weight range	Approximate age range	Group stage/type of seat
birth–10kg (0–22lb)	newborn to 9 months	0 rear-facing
birth–13kg (0–29lb)	newborn to 15-18 months	0+ rear-facing
9–18kg (20–40lb)	9 months to 3-4 years	1 forward-facing
15–25kg (20lb–3st 13lb)	up to 6 years	2 booster seat
22–36kg (3st 7lb–5st 9lb)	up to 11 years	3 booster seat

 For information about child car seats and other road safety information visit www.childcarseats.org.uk and www.thinkroadsafety.gov.uk.

Take the stage

Retailers often describe child car seats in stages:

Stage 1: Groups 0 and 0+
Stage 2: Group 1
Stage 3: Group 2
Stage 4: Group 3

 Do not use rear-facing car seats on front passenger seats fitted with an airbag unless it has been deactivated. In the event of a crash, the airbag could result in the serious injury or death of the child.

SEAT TYPES AND SIZES

You will probably need to buy two or three different car seats, as your child grows. There are three types of car seat for babies and toddlers: rear-facing baby seats, forward-facing seats and multi-group seats. Booster seats, which simply raise the child up so the adult belt can be safely worn, are used for older children. Some seats are designed to stay in the car, while others are lighter and more portable. Read about your choices over the next few pages.

Rear-facing baby seats

These are designed for babies up to 13kg (29lb) (up to about 15–18 months), depending on the model of seat. They are rear-facing and can be fitted in the front (unless there is an airbag, see box, above) or rear and are held in place by the adult seat belt while your baby is secured to the seat using an integral safety harness. These seats are designed to support a young baby's vulnerable back and neck in the event of an accident, and are classified as either

Keep your child in a rear-facing seat for as long as possible, until either he or she is above the maximum weight for the seat, or the top of his or her head is above the top of the seat. It does not matter if knees are bent in the seat, provided your baby is within the seat's weight range.

« Rear-facing car seats are designed to support a young baby's vulnerable back and neck in the event of an accident. »

115

The pros and cons of rear-facing baby seats

Pros	Cons
• You can use the seat to carry your baby to and from the car • It can be a useful additional baby chair for the home • Some can be adjusted to have a rocking motion when placed on the floor – helpful for soothing your baby (they provide more support than a reclined cradle and are suitable for short naps) • Some are part of a travel system (see pages 144–6)	• Don't expect it to double up as an extra baby carrier other than to transport your baby to and from the car - it is a fairly heavy piece of equipment and once your baby is past the newborn stage you'll be aching to put it down

group 0 or 0+ (see table, page 114). Baby seats have a carrying handle so you can transport your baby to and from the car easily, and most have a rocking facility for use in the home. Some models fit onto a pushchair chassis as part of a travel system (see pages 144–6).

New babies can look scrunched-up and uncomfortable because these seats are rarely designed to recline. For safety reasons, the seat shouldn't be shifted to lie in a flatter position while in the car unless it has been specifically designed to allow this. However, a head-support cushion can help.

Harnesses

Group 0 and Group 1 seats for younger children generally have a three- or a five-point harness built into the child seat. Group 2 and 3 seats and booster seats generally don't have this, but use the car's normal three-point adult seat belt to secure the child in the seat. In general, a five-point harness is more effective at restraining a child because, with a three-point belt, the shoulder belt can slip in a crash if it's not correctly positioned.

 For more consumer advice about car seats, go to the Which? website at www.which.co.uk.

Forward-facing seats

Once your child weighs at least 9kg (20lb) (about nine months) and can sit unaided, he or she can use a forward-facing seat (although your child should stay in a rear-facing seat for as long as possible, see box, page 115). These seats are for older babies and children up to about 25kg (3st 13lb) (age three to seven years), depending on the seat, and are classified in groups 1 and 2. Unlike rear-facing seats, they are designed to be left in the car most of the time. Children weighing up to 18kg (40lb) are secured using an integral harness. From 18kg to 36kg (40lb to 5st 9lb) the adult diagonal and lap belts are used.

Some seats are available with pull-out drink and snack holders, which can be really useful on long journeys. Of course it is not possible for a driver to have safe eye-contact with a child seated in the back of the car, so you may want to consider a special mirror (see pages 125–6).

❝ Unlike rear-facing seats, forward-facing ones are designed to be left in the car most of the time and make use of adult diagonal and lap belts. ❞

The pros and cons of forward-facing seats

Pros	Cons
● Reclining options mean they can be more comfortable, especially on long journeys	● These seats are generally designed to stay in the car – so can restrict space if, for example, you don't have your child with you and need to give other people a lift
● Models that enable you to remove the harness and use the adult belt for older children are more versatile because older children might find a harness over-restricting	● Not designed to be portable
● Many have a high sitting position – good for relieving boredom in smaller children by enabling them to see out of the car window, and sometimes helpful for children who suffer car sickness	

Multi-group seats

Also known as 'combination' seats, these can be positioned to be either rear-facing for a young baby, or forward-facing for a child who can sit unaided. They can be used from birth until your child weighs about 18kg (40lb) (about age three to four years). The seat is semi-permanently attached to the interior of the car using the adult seat belt, and an integral harness secures the child into the seat. Most harnesses can be tightened with one pull, so they are quite easy to use. The seats have adjustable seat-recline positions for sleeping and the height of the head restraint can also be adjusted.

 These seats have not performed well in Which? safety tests and are not a good choice because, as a child's bone and body structure changes, so do the safety restraint requirements, and one seat cannot meet them all.

" A multi-group seat is semi-permanently attached to the car. "

The pros and cons of multi-group seats

Pros	Cons
• In theory, you shouldn't need to buy another seat until your child is ready to move on to a booster seat (see box, below) • The reclining positions help to make the car ride more comfortable for a sleepy child	• During the baby-months, these seats are not as portable or versatile as a baby seat – for example, you can't easily move the seat to carry a sleeping baby to and from the car • Older children may find some models restrictive and you could end up forking out for another type of seat earlier than you expected

Converting to booster seats

Some car seats can be converted to a booster seat as they have a detachable back that is removed once the child grows big enough.

Remember that the level of side-crash protection from most booster seats isn't as good as that which is available from many full seats.

Points to consider before buying: Car seats

The car seat is a crucial purchase and you should consider the following points when making your decision:

Your child's weight, rather than his or her age, is the determining factor when buying or using a car seat.

If yours is a one-car family, the chances are, once installed, your second car seat will hardly ever move. However, if you're going to be transferring your seat between two cars, or using the seat regularly in other people's cars, portability is a key issue (assuming you don't buy two seats). So choose a model that is lightweight and easy to install.

Go for removable, machine-washable covers – the seat will get dirty and machine washing is the best way of keeping the covers clean.

Make a list of the cars in which you might use the child seat – for example, friends' or grandparents' – as well as your own. Check if the seat will fit.

Think about whether you'll need to use the seat with a lap belt in the centre of the rear seat in any of these cars. Not all seats are designed for this. Generally, it's best to use a standard three-point seat belt (or Isofix system, see page 121) if you can.

Check with the sales staff that the seat you want is compatible with the make and model of your car. There is no industry standard, which means there is no child seat that fits all cars – although most models will fit most cars. Your best option is to buy at a shop that will 'test install' the seat to make sure it fits your car.

SAFETY CONCERNS

Which? has criticised the official safety test that manufacturers have to put their seats through before they are allowed on to the European market. It says the current test (referred to by its legal requirement of ECE 44/03 or 04) mimics a fairly unrealistic and undemanding front-impact crash. And, surprisingly, there is no requirement for child car seats to pass a side-impact test, despite the fact that side impacts are the second most common type of crash (often occurring at junctions).

Which? tested seats for both front and side impacts replicating more true-to-life conditions of what happens to a car in an extreme crash. The results of the tests

 For more details on car seat safety, see www.which.co.uk.

119

highlighted some weaknesses in child car seats that would never show up in the standard tests used to certify a seat as safe for sale.

So where does this leave parents who want to buy a safe car seat for their child? It is important to bear in mind that many crashes happen at a lower speed than that at which the seats were tested by Which?, and that any properly fitted seat will offer far better protection than not using one at all. Fitting the right size of seat for your car and for your child is a crucial safety measure – experts say that most child deaths in car crashes are caused by seats that haven't been fitted properly, and could be avoided if people bought the right seat for the car and took time to read the instructions and get to know how the seat works. Read the section below on choosing, fitting and using car seats for advice on this.

> " Any properly fitted seat will offer far better protection than not using one at all. Fitting the right size of seat for your car and your child is a crucial safety measure. "

FITTING CORRECTLY AND MAINTAINING SAFETY

Some car seats are easier to fit properly in your car than others. You must make sure you fit your seat properly. Even if you've bought the safest car seat on the market, if you haven't fitted it correctly, your baby is at risk.

Ask for a demonstration. Make sure you have a go at fitting the seat yourself, too, before you buy.

Follow the instructions carefully when fitting the seat yourself and keep a copy of the instructions in the car. Don't buy the seat if you find the instructions hard to understand. Providing clear instructions is a basic but critical measure that all manufacturers should be getting right.

Practise fitting the seat a few times before you use it.

Make sure the child seat fits firmly on to the car seat – there should be very little forward or sideways movement. When you open the buckle of the adult belt, a correctly installed seat should spring forward slightly.

Be careful not to push the seat too hard into the car – for example, by pushing it down with your knee. This could damage the seat.

Bear in mind other people who will be using the seat – for example, grandparents. If there's anything awkward about fitting the seat, will they be able to install it correctly? Make sure you show them how to fit it properly.

If the seat has a harness, make sure it is correctly adjusted every time you use it – only one or two fingers should fit between your child's chest and the harness. Position the harness buckle over the hips, not over the stomach.

If a diagonal seat belt is used, this should rest on the child's shoulder, not on his or her neck.

The seat-belt buckle should be straight when locked. It should not rest on the car-seat frame as this may cause it to snap open in an accident.

Exposed metal fittings can get very hot on a sunny day. Keep a blanket in the car to cover the seat when it is not being used.

Never modify the seat – for example, by adding extra padding.

Go for Isofix

Isofix is a secure fitting method for child car seats using two metal catches welded to the car body. An Isofix seat latches on to these catches and a third support is provided either by a 'leg' at the front (which rests on the floor of the car), or a 'top tether' strap at the back. Using Isofix means there is no need to use the car seat belt, and the risk of incorrect fitting is very low. Isofix seats are becoming more widely available, so if you have an Isofix mount in your car, you may feel an Isofix seat is a good safety option. However, don't assume your Isofix car will suit all Isofix seats: some cars have a 'false floor', which won't work with a support leg.

If you have an accident, buy a new seat – the existing one may have been damaged, even if this isn't visible.

Secure your child properly for every journey, no matter how short.

Know your place

The safest place for a child's car seat is the centre of the rear seat (this way it is protected from side impact). If it is not possible to put the seat here, an outside rear seat is the next best option. The front passenger seat should be your last choice, although many parents find it more practical to have a young baby next to them rather than behind them. Baby seats and portable forward-facing seats are suitable for use in both the front or back of the car; and combination and fixed forward-facing seats can generally be used in the front seat, but this depends on the model of car seat.

Car seats and the law

New car seat legislation came into force in September 2006. In summary:

Under three years or up to 90cm (3ft)	Up to 135cm (4ft 5in)	Over 135cm (4ft 5in)
Front seat		
Appropriate child restraint must be used	Appropriate child restraint must be used	Seat belt must be worn if fitted
Rear seat		
Appropriate child restraint must be used*	Appropriate child restraint must be used	Seat belt must be worn if available*

* The only exceptions are in taxis; on 'emergency' (unplanned) journeys where an appropriate restraint is not available, or where two occupied child seats in the rear prevent the fitting of a third child seat. In these cases, your child should use the adult seat belt.

HIRE CAR SEATS

If you hire a car on holiday and can't take a baby car seat with you (or it doesn't fit), you'll have to hire one. This should be simple, but Which? researchers found worrying problems when they hired child car seats from a range of car-hire companies in the UK, Greece and Spain. Many of the seats provided were so out of date they didn't meet modern safety standards. Some had bits broken through wear and tear. Where the hire outlets fitted the seats for the researchers, they were often fitted incorrectly. Many outlets, especially those in the UK, expect you to fit the seat yourself but the Which? researchers found they often failed to provide adequate instructions to enable parents to fit the seat properly.

Children's lives are being put at risk because of these practices by hire companies. Which? has taken up the issue with the trade body representing car-hire companies in the UK. If you're not happy with the seat provided by your car-hire company, it is safest to buy a new seat yourself at your destination. Although this is an expensive option, new seats for sale have to pass modern safety tests so you'll be protecting your baby properly. If this isn't an option for you, bear in mind that any seat is better than no seat at all.

‘‘If you're not happy with a seat provided by a car-hire company, buy a new seat. ’’

CHILD SEATS ON PLANES

The safest way for a child aged between six months and two years to travel on a plane is using a child restraint – either a car seat provided by you or a restraint provided by the airline. This is the theory. The reality is that your car seat will not necessarily be suitable for use on the plane, and not all airlines provide their own restraints. Sitting on their parent's lap with a loop-extension belt, which is what a lot of young children end up doing, is second best in terms of safety. Children between the ages of two and three years must sit in their own seat with a special belt, or in a child restraint. Babies under six months old are too small to sit in a separate seat, so generally must sit on your lap – although some airlines have a limited number of baby 'cradles' fitted in specific sections of the plane. Once your child is three, there are no special requirements.

If you are travelling on a plane with a child under three, talk through the seating options with the airline or travel agent before you depart. If you are planning to use a car seat on board, check that it will be suitable for use on the plane. Tell the airline that you will be wanting a child restraint when you book your tickets – if you just turn up, there may not be enough available on the plane.

Another option when flying is to buy your own restraint. There is one called a 'flight vest', which allows your baby to sit on your lap and also be properly restrained.

The safest way for a child aged between six months and two years to travel on a plane is in a car seat provided by you or a restraint provided by the airline.

Car accessories

There can't be many parents of babies and young children who have avoided the experience of a car journey from hell, although there are things that can help.

Although a gently humming engine has wonderful sleep-inducing powers, especially in the early months, a bored, grouchy or mischievous child strapped into the back can easily turn a run-of-the-mill journey into a stress-filled rollercoaster ride. Toys can become missiles, supposedly secure seat belts get undone, crying can seem non-stop and there is always the threat of a projectile vomit or a particularly unfortunate 'toilet accident' in the middle of a rush-hour traffic jam.

Some of these situations are more or less unavoidable, and parents can only try their utmost to stay cool, calm and collected in the most trying of conditions. For others, however, manufacturers have come up with a range of products designed to help alleviate the stress of fretful journeys. Gadgets range from rear-view mirrors, so you can see what is going on in the back without having to turn around, to glorious sleep-inducing comfort cushions.

❝ Gadgets for the car range from rear-view mirrors, so you can see what is going on in the back, to sleep-inducing comfort cushions. ❞

A CAR SURVIVAL KIT

As a starting point, it is worth putting together your own 'car survival kit' that you keep in the car permanently, making sure you renew the contents as and when necessary. All this needs to contain are a few basic items that you feel could be useful to you in some situations. Obviously the contents will vary depending on the child's needs and age, but a selection along the following lines could prove handy surprisingly often:

- Spare nappies
- A packet of wipes
- Nappy sacks
- Muslin cloth or small towel (especially useful as a quickly grabbable cleaning aid after a bout of sickness)
- Snacks (but nothing your child could choke on)
- Spare dummies
- A couple of picture books and toys
- A change of clothes (and maybe a spare top for you too).

Some items can be packed away in the boot or in a bag, but others, such as the snacks or the dummies, you will want to keep within arm's reach.

OTHER CAR ACCESSORIES

Think about your own and your child's needs and foibles before you fork out on a range of car accessories. In that way, you may be able to avoid having a car stuffed with supposedly innovative and 'essential' items that are simply ignored or abused.

Seat-belt safety

Your baby could easily turn into a seat-belt escapee once he or she has the curiosity and dexterity to work out the seat-belt mechanism. There are products designed to make undoing the seat-belt buckle more difficult, such as a plastic see-through clip that slides over the seat-belt buckle – when you want to undo the buckle, you slide the clip out of the way.

Other seat-belt products are designed to improve the fit of the belt, such as a ratchet mechanism device that allows you easily to tighten slack on seat belts securing a car seat.

Sunblinds

Car sunblinds can be very useful for helping children sleep on bright days and simply for stopping the sun from shining in their eyes. You usually attach the sunblinds to the side back window, using either suction pads or clips. Some models are designed like household blinds and can be rolled up when you don't need to use them. Others are simply taken on and off the window as and when needed. Those that use suction pads need to be placed on a clean window

 Make sure that you check the suction pads regularly and if they show signs of breaking into small pieces, stop using the blind. All sunblinds can provide a certain level of amusement if within reach of curious fingers, so they may not be as durable or stay up for as long as you might hope.

otherwise the pads may not stick. You can also buy sun canopies that fit over infant car seats.

Sleep cushions

Cushioned neck rolls can prevent your child's head from lolling from side to side when he or she is in a deep slumber. Some of these come in the form of cuddly toys so may also provide a degree of entertainment. The main drawback is that some children don't like wearing them. Neck cushions are widely available from children's stores.

You can also buy support cushions for older children who use a booster seat, such as a cushion 'roll' that fits over the seat belt in a position that comfortably enables your child to rest his or her head against the cushion.

Rear-view mirrors

Turning around when you are driving, because your baby has made an unfamiliar sound or your toddler is

Travelling with your baby

125

complaining, is an understandable but very dangerous response that a rear-view mirror can help you avoid. Depending on the model, you can fit this over your existing mirror or position it with suction pads in an appropriate place on the windscreen. Some give you a panoramic view of the traffic behind and are usually made up of one wide mirror for the traffic with a smaller one directed at the back seat. Others are designed to give you a view of just the back seat. Don't expect a perfect view of your child, however – it depends where in the back your child is sitting, and front-seat headrests can partially obscure the view.

❝ Some rear-view mirrors give you a panoramic view of the traffic behind with a smaller one directed at the back seat. ❞

Staying snug

You can, of course, just use a good old spare blanket – but, needless to say, a range of products are available for keeping your baby cosy on cold car journeys. You can buy a wide range of fleeces and blankets that fit into or over a car seat. You can also buy covers to protect your baby from the wind or rain while being carried along in the car seat. These are normally designed to fit baby car seats with rigid handles. They are widely available from children's stores.

Keeping clean

Sticky fingers and grubby shoes will soon turn the car into a pit. You could put up with it and have a clean-up whenever you get the chance, or you could be extra-vigilant and try to ensure that faces and fingers are wiped, shoes are removed and food and drink are banned before putting your children in the car. Alternatively, you could buy some car interior 'protectors'. These are wipe-clean bits of plastic of various shapes and forms designed to shield your seats. You can also buy large wipe-clean mats that fit under and around your child's seat, ensuring that he or she is surrounded by a cleanable zone. To protect your seats from toilet accidents and drinks spills, you can buy absorbent, stay-dry cushions that fit into a car seat.

Food and drink

You can buy car bottle-warmers, which plug into the car cigarette lighter (see page 92). For older children, there are special food and drink holders that you attach to the door or to the back of the front seat so (theoretically at least) children can rest their drinks without spilling them and save half-eaten snacks for later rather than letting them drop on the floor.

Storage solutions

There are various storage products to help keep under control the mass of toys, books and other bits and pieces that can easily build up in your car when you have children. A car tidy or organiser, for example, fits over a front seat headrest and has a range of different-sized pockets for all your essentials. These are useful for older children or if you are sitting in the back with your child and want to have everything within reach. They are not particularly handy, however, when you are in the front. Try car accessory shops for these items.

One storage item you won't need to spend money on is a simple bag for rubbish – having a bag to throw everything into, particularly on long car journeys, can give you at least some sense of order. You can buy special car litter containers that fit over the front-seat headrest but a plastic bag will do the job perfectly well, provided it is kept well out of the child's reach as it is, of course, a safety hazard.

In-car toys and entertainment

If your child has a favourite toy, it's worth making sure you have it at hand on car journeys. Some toys, however, are designed specifically for travel use. Because babies tend to drop their toys and cry to get them back, many of these car toys can be attached to your child's seat or the car interior, or to your child. The following are some examples.

- **Mini baby gyms** – several manufacturers produce colourful characters attached to a padded bar, which you place over the car seat within easy reach for patting and tweaking.
- **Velcro-fastening rattles** are handy for the car because the rattle, usually in

the form of a soft animal, is attached to a Velcro band that you put around your baby's wrist. Your baby can't drop the rattle and should have fun waving his or her arms around to make the rattle 'rattle'.

- **Shake, rattle and roll toys** – a selection of colourful soft animal-shaped toys that you 'hook' on to a car seat canopy.
- **Suction toys** – you can buy a range of toys that stick to the car window within reach of your baby.

If toys don't seem to do the trick, music tapes or CDs or – for older children – simple story tapes can be good entertainment value. Another option is to fit an in-car DVD player, which allows you to hang a screen (or screens) on the seatback, allowing children to watch films as you cruise. They can use earphones if you don't want the distraction of the soundtrack as you drive. If your car isn't fitted with one, you can buy or hire this potentially valuable boredom-killer.

❝ The day you'll know for certain that you have children is when you put on the children's music tapes or CDs - and your children aren't even travelling with you. ❞

127

Baby carriers

When your baby is small, a baby carrier, or sling, is a useful way of going out and about with minimal hassle. With both hands free and without having to manage a pram or pushchair, you'll have more freedom to undertake such delights as the shopping, negotiating public transport and loading up the car.

If you have a toddler as well as a baby, you can go out with the carrier and the buggy, avoiding – or at least postponing – the need to buy a double pushchair. Even when you are in the house, a carrier can prove handy. Babies are often soothed by being so close to a warm body, so you can use the carrier to calm your baby while you are doing the housework (but not the cooking) or gardening.

Bear in mind that some babies simply don't like baby carriers. This is less the case when they are very young, but once they start becoming mobile, the protests at being 'harnessed' into a carrier can start. Consider this if you are thinking of buying a model designed to cope with a wide age range (some can carry a compliant child well into the toddler years). Unfortunately, there's no way of knowing how your older baby will take to a carrier – it's a case of buy before you try. Remember, too, that your movement and balance will be affected and that however well designed a carrier is, depending on your own stature and the weight of your baby, using one may simply become more and more uncomfortable for you as your

baby grows. Having said that, many parents continue to find carriers a useful additional mode of transport for older babies and toddlers.

TYPES OF BABY CARRIER

There are three main carrier types available, the major difference between these being the various positions in which they enable you to carry your baby. See page 130 for the pros and cons of each of the following types.

Soft carriers

These are the simplest carriers. Most are two-way carriers that will let you carry your baby facing you – most suited to very young babies – or facing outwards to view the world. For babies who cannot support their heads, the carrier should have a padded headrest that can normally be folded down for an older baby. Leg holes should also be adjustable – the smaller the baby, the smaller the hole. For the ultimate in flexibility, look out for a soft carrier that converts into a changing bag. All soft carriers are generally suitable for babies up to about nine months.

Multi-way carriers

With this type, depending on the model, in addition to being able to carry your baby upright on your front, you can carry him or her in a nursing, or 'cradle' position; on your back; or at your side, 'hipster' style.

Many models offer just three positions – usually to carry your baby on your front, back or in a nursing position. Four-way carriers let your baby go on your front or back, or in the nursing or hip position.

Most multi-way carriers are of a similar design to the soft carrier and have a 'harness'-style appearance. Others are more like traditional slings and are hammock-style: a large piece of thick fabric holds your baby and continues around your shoulders –

you adjust the sling by pulling the fabric through a pair of strong plastic rings. Some may be no more than a circular band of material or a long piece of material wound around the body and tied with a knot.

Multi-way carriers tend to be designed for babies from birth to either 12 months, 18 months or to a 14kg (31lb) toddler, depending on the model.

Framed carriers

These carriers are generally aimed at babies from six months, because they need to be able to support themselves sitting up. The carriers have a rucksack-style appearance: your baby sits in a harness, supported either by a lightweight metal frame or rigid rucksack-style padding, and the carrier is put on using padded shoulder straps and a waist belt. Your baby will be positioned with his or her head and shoulders just above your shoulders.

Those models at the top end of the market are made by outdoor clothing and equipment specialists. Some have a fair amount of storage space, for clothing and food, for example, and with some models you can buy extras such as sun and rain covers. As long as your child is willing, and your back can take it, you can use most models until the age of two-and-a-half or three.

! Slings that carry the baby across your body are available. Some designs may not enable you to keep an eye on your baby as their bodies are almost covered in the sling. There could also be a risk of overheating the baby as the majority of his or her body is covered.

When travelling with your baby, a travel cot is a valuable piece of kit. In this book, travel cot information is given in the section on furnishing the nursery (see pages 49–51).

The pros and cons of baby carriers

Soft carriers

Pros	Cons
• Two positions are sufficient for most parents and younger babies • Tend to be cheaper than the alternatives	• Not as versatile as other carriers

Multi-way carriers

Pros	Cons
• More versatile than two-way carriers • Longer lifespan • Those offering a nursing position can be particularly handy for breast-feeding	• Tend to be more expensive than soft carriers • Some, particularly the sling style, can take a bit of practice to use correctly (a few brands come with instructional videos) • Lifespan may be limited by the recalcitrance of an older baby or toddler

Framed carriers

Pros	Cons
• The above-the-shoulder position is popular with babies and toddlers because they are high enough to get a grown-up view of the world (the back position of the fabric multi-way carriers, in contrast, tends to be lower down, so your baby's view is restricted) • Parents who want regularly to take their child on walks or hikes can get carriers designed specifically with their needs in mind – for example, extra-lightweight and comfortable carriers with weatherproof features • Carriers with a metal frame are usually designed so you can stand the carrier upright on its own – making it easier to get your child in and out and useful for standing the carrier up on its own when you need a rest (although you must not leave your child unattended in a carrier)	• Be prepared for pain! – some babies will never tire of pulling your hair and ears from their superb hard-for-you-to-reach vantage position at the back (using a sun/rain cover is one way of ensuring this doesn't happen) • You may well need another person around to help you put the carrier on and take it off, so it might not be ideal for use on your own – unless you find it manageable to put on and take off by resting it on a seat • Tend to be the most expensive type of carrier available – although you can get basic models that are fine for strolls, the top-of-the-range models aimed at serious walkers are not cheap • Need to allow extra head space when going through doorways, under trees, etc.

Points to consider before buying: Baby carriers

A baby carrier can be a really useful purchase, but it needs to be right for everyone who'll use it – wearers and baby. These points will help:

You need to feel secure and comfortable with your baby in the carrier. If you can, try out a selection of carriers with your baby in them to see which feels most comfortable for you.

Even if you can't try out carriers with your baby inside, try a selection on anyway to see how you get on with fastening devices and position adjustments. If anything seems over-fiddly to you or if you think you'll have trouble putting a carrier on properly, move on to another one (although bear in mind that some types simply need a bit of practice to get right).

Look for shoulder straps that are wide and well-padded.

Your baby needs comfort too – if there are leg holes, check these are well-padded and that there is also good support and padding for your baby's back and – for younger babies in particular – head.

Think about whether you need a carrier with added 'bits and bobs', such as a 'soother pouch' or a 'dribble bib' – some models have these and you may find them useful.

Check whether the carrier is machine-washable. It is bound to get dribbled or vomited on at some point, so anything that is sponge-clean only won't stay as fresh as one that you can simply throw in the washing machine.

If you intend to spend a lot of time outdoors with your baby in a carrier, choose one that has a canopy to protect his or her head from the sun.

Metal parts (as in framed carriers) can get uncomfortably hot or cold depending on the weather.

131

Cycling with your baby

If you used a bike a lot for transport before you had your baby, there's no reason to stop using it after he or she is born. As long as you have the right equipment, cycling with your baby can be a quick and convenient way of getting out and about.

You may have to wait a while, however. For obvious safety reasons, it's not recommended that you take a baby who cannot support his or her own head out with you on a bike – as until this time he or she won't be able to wear a cycling helmet. Ideally, your baby should also be able to sit well and unaided. Baby bike seats tend to be designed for use by babies from about six months of age. Trailers, designed to carry one or two children, are also available.

Whichever option you are interested in, check with the bike retailer that your bike is suitable for use with a child seat or trailer, as not all bike designs are appropriate.

 Wearing a cycle helmet reduces the risk of head injury by 85% and the risk of brain injury by almost 90%. You and your child should always wear helmets when on a bike.

TYPES OF BICYCLE SEATS AND TRAILERS

Once your baby is old enough to go with you on your bike, you have a choice from the seat options outlined on these pages and overleaf.

Rear-mounted seats

Rear-mounted seats are the most widely used bike seats. They fit over the back wheel and will usually constitute a high back and raised sides, leg guards and a safety harness.

❝ As long as you have the right equipment, cycling with your baby can be a quick and convenient way of getting out about. ❞

Front-mounted seats

With this type of seat, your child sits in front of you and you place your arms around the seat and child to hold the handlebars. Because your arms have to go around the seat and your vision of the road needs to be clear, front-mounted seats are more compact than rear-mounted seats.

❝ Ideally, your baby should be able to sit up well and unaided before venturing out on a bicycle together. Helmets are crucial for you both. ❞

The pros and cons of bicycle seats

Rear-mounted seats

Pros	Cons
• High back and sides mean that younger children are well supported if they want to go to sleep while you are cycling • You can use the seat to carry shopping when you don't have your child with you	• Carrying extra weight on the back of the bike, especially if your child is moving around, can make stability a problem • You can't see what your child is up to or talk to him or her very easily while you are cycling

Front-mounted seats

Pros	Cons
• You have closer contact with your child, so can chat with and have better control of him or her as you are cycling • Stability can be easier to maintain on a front-mounted seat because the extra weight is at the front	• Although popular in mainland Europe, these seats are less generally available in the UK than rear-mounted seats and may be hard to find (see box, below)

 If you have difficulty finding front-mounted seats in conventional bicycle stores, try bike specialists such as www.realcycles.com or www.kidsonthemove.co.uk.

Bicycle trailers

With these, you tow your child behind you in an enclosed 'carriage'. They have two bicycle-type wheels and a long hitching arm that fastens to your bike. Your child is seated and strapped in inside the zippered, weatherproof and ventilated compartment, which has fabric or plastic windows so that he or she can see out as you are cycling.

The pros and cons of bicycle trailers

Pros	Cons
• Your child should have a decent amount of space inside the trailer, with reasonable leg room, comfy seating and storage places for toys • Two-seaters are widely available, so you can cycle with two small children • You will probably feel more stable cycling with a trailer than with a bike seat because the extra weight isn't directly on the bike • With some makes you can buy a special handle attachment to convert the trailer into a pushchair	• You won't have the same physical closeness to your child as you would with a bike seat • Although any trailer used on the road should have a tall pennant and rear lighting so that it is clearly visible to motorists, the fact that your child is seated at quite a low level can make him or her appear vulnerable, and you may feel happier using the trailer 'off road' – for example, in a park – rather than as a practical travel solution to get from A to B • Trailers can tip over, especially when turning abruptly or going over bumps • They can be expensive and you will need to consider whether you will use the trailer enough to justify the price

Holidays with a baby

When you first go on holiday with your baby, you'll be amazed at all the extra baggage you find yourself taking with you. From travel cots to favourite toys or blankets ... the list of items can go on and on unless you sit down and think about what you really need and what you can do without for a couple of weeks.

STAYING SAFE IN THE SUN

It is vital that you protect your baby's skin from the sun. Small babies need to be kept out of the sun completely. It is harder to do this with toddlers and babies on the move, so you need to be vigilant. Use the following:

Sun hat

This is essential for sun protection. With older babies or toddlers you'll probably have to wrestle with them to keep it on their head, so a hat with ties or an elasticated fit can help to resist determined little hands. 'Legionnaire' styles with a flap at the back are widely available and are very effective at protecting the whole head and neck. Wide-brimmed hats are a good alternative. Other styles – for example, a straightforward baseball cap design – won't provide the necessary protection.

Sun-safe clothing

At its most basic, this means long-sleeves and trousers not shorts. However, for periods of long exposure, this often isn't enough to protect a child's skin from burning as clothing can still let through some harmful ultraviolet (UV) rays. If you want to be sure of maximum protection, you can buy special clothes that guarantee to let through only the tiniest amounts of UV rays. Look for clothes with the label 'prevents sunburn'. Clothes with this claim will have reached British Standard 7949, which sets a strict sun protection standard for children's clothes.

Sun cream

Choose a cream with a sun protection factor (SPF) of 15–30. Many sun creams aimed at children will have an SPF higher than 30, but they won't actually give your child much more protection in real terms. A 20-point increase in the SPF number doesn't give a corresponding increase in protection. There is concern that buying sun creams with a higher SPF than 30 lulls parents into a false sense of security about how long their children can be exposed to the sun – in Australia, for example, 30+ is the highest SPF allowed – and Which? believes that SPF labels above 30 should be banned in the UK too.

(Continued on page 138)

Travelling tips

These points will help ensure your trip goes smoothly.

Check what equipment is available at your destination

Check what baby equipment the company you are travelling with, or the place you are travelling to, can provide. If you are hiring a cottage, for example, items such as highchairs and cots are often provided and, if not, you can normally hire such equipment through the holiday home company. If you are travelling abroad with a tour operator, you will probably be able to hire cots and even buggies through them, as many pride themselves on the baby-friendliness of their resorts. Alternatively, you can contact the local tourist office.

Decide if you need to take every last piece of equipment

You don't need everything you use at home and you can make substitutions – for example, you could use the child car seat as a feeding chair, or a baby carrier instead of a pushchair for getting out and about; and use boiling water in a pan instead of a space-consuming steriliser for sterilising bottles (see pages 87–9).

Borrow rather than buy

If you don't want to increase your holiday budget, this can be a good way around it. If you know someone with a travel cot or a spare, lightweight buggy, for example, there's no harm in asking.

Consider taking disposable items

Disposable items of baby equipment, although not particularly environmentally friendly, can make your life easier on holiday – see pages 85 and 109 for details of disposable bottles and bibs and, if you normally use washable nappies, see pages 16–18 for details of disposable nappies.

Buy a cheaper model

If you do decide to buy new, bear in mind that you'll probably only be using the item(s) occasionally after your holiday, so basic rather than top-of-the-range is likely to be adequate. A possible exception to this is if you are buying your first umbrella-folding stroller (see pages 140-1) to go on holiday. There's a fair chance that you will be using this regularly at some point, once you or your baby 'grow out of' your current mode of pushchair transport. The most basic strollers, although fine as a spare, tend to be less user-friendly than the slightly more sophisticated models. Paying a little bit more for a lighter-weight model with a few extra features is worth considering.

Buy travel models

Travel versions of various types of baby equipment are widely available (although think hard whether you really need to buy) – see pages 49–51 for details of travel cots/playpens, pages 90 and 92 for travel sterilisers and travel bottle-warmers, and page 181 for travel potties.

Plan nappy supplies

The most popular nappy brands are available in most foreign resorts, so if you need to restrict your luggage it's worth buying them once you get there. However, they can be more expensive than in the UK. If you're travelling abroad by car, in particular, consider taking a full supply of nappies with you.

> **Think through your requirements well in advance of your trip and plan accordingly. All should then go according to plan.**

It's also worth avoiding very cheap, little-known creams: tests by trading standards officers and Which? have found some of these to have far lower levels of sun protection than is claimed on the label. Stick to well-known brands (or, for good value for money for the same level of protection, own-label chain-store products), and buy before you travel: suncreams purchased abroad may not meet these demanding requirements and may be mis-labelled.

OTHER BEACH ACCESSORIES

There are a few other possible products that might make life better when you've got sand between your toes.

Swim nappies

There are two types of these – reusable and disposable. They are useful if you don't want your child in normal nappies on the beach and don't want to risk any 'accidents' in the water. They have a sewn-in nylon mesh to keep poo inside. Travel companies and hotels will often insist that non-toilet-trained children wear swim nappies in swimming pools, and ordinary trunks and swimming costumes will not be acceptable.

Swim nappies with ties or side-snap fastenings will be easier to change than pull-on-and-off styles. It's best to buy two reusable swim nappies so one can dry while the other is in use. You can also buy packs of disposable swim nappies (available from most supermarkets), although these can work out expensive and a fairly bulky item to take away with you if you need to minimise your luggage.

Baby wetsuits

These allow your baby to stay playing in the water for longer. They open at the bottom for easy changing.

Buoyancy aids

Older children can have armbands but babies needn't miss out on the joys of floating in the water. You can buy baby swim floats, which have an integral shaped baby seat with leg holes. Your baby sits in the seat with his or her back and chest supported and can splash about and kick safely (with, of course, an adult keeping the child within arm's reach). Buoyancy aids come in different sizes and are suitable for babies from about three months. They are widely available.

Sun-safe tents/cabanas

These pop-up, pod-shaped, open-sided tents are ideal for keeping a young baby properly in the shade when on the beach, and offer high levels of UV protection. You can buy family-sized as well as child-sized tents so that adults can sit in the shade too. They are widely available from nursery and department stores.

If you go away on holiday, take a first-aid kit with you so that you know you have important items readily to hand. See pages 160-1 for details.

Pushchairs

Single or double seater? Foldable or all-terrain? Three or four wheels? The seemingly simple choice of how you will keep your baby comfortable as you wheel him or her to the park has never been more complicated. This chapter steers you through the selection route to help you find the 'first set of wheels' for your child.

What do you need?

A pushchair is a bit like a car - any one will get you there in reasonable comfort, but you will pay more for something with good suspension, luxury padded seating and fashionable styling.

There are many varieties of pushchair, and the pros and cons of the main different types are covered in this chapter. Perfectly acceptable buggy-style pushchairs, suitable from birth, can be found at reasonable prices, but you can pay more for a top-of-the-range version or a fashionable three-wheeler. Your baby will probably be happy in whatever model you choose (as long as it's designed to be used from birth – see box, page 142), but your own needs are also very important.

"Retailers categorise pushchairs in many different ways, but all products fall into the following categories: lightweight stroller, pushchair, all-terrain or travel system."

TYPES OF PUSHCHAIR

There are four main types of pushchair: lightweight strollers (or buggies), pushchairs, all-terrain and travel systems, each of which are covered in this section.

Manufacturers and retailers categorise pushchairs in many different ways, but all products fall into one of these categories, and some straddle more than one type. For example, a three-wheeled pushchair with pneumatic wheels that can be used with a car seat is both all-terrain and a travel system.

Strollers

Also known as buggies, these are lightweight pushchairs that fold up quickly and easily into a relatively flat shape ('umbrella folding'). The best ones can be folded with one hand, an invaluable feature for a parent out alone with their child. Some strollers do not provide sufficient back support for babies less than three or four months old,

 For more consumer advice about pushchairs, go to the Which? website at www.which.co.uk.

although some models can be used from birth. Others don't recline at all and these shouldn't be used until your baby is six to nine months old.

While they are ideal for day-to-day use, many strollers aren't good for bumpy journeys because of their small, hard plastic wheels and lack of suspension. However, if you use public transport or hop on and off planes for holidays, a lightweight, easy-folding, compact pushchair is ideal. Some come with more features than others – for example, a multi-position seat, removable washable covers or an inclusive rain cover and hood – and the price reflects this. The essential requirements are that they are easy to push, steer and fold, and comfortable for your child.

> **❝ What used to be known as a buggy is increasingly sold by retailers as a stroller. ❞**

The pros and cons of strollers or buggies

Pros	Cons
• The most versatile type of pushchair for older babies and toddlers – their light weight and ease of folding means you can take them just about anywhere	• The simplest, cheapest models lack features that are likely to be useful, such as lockable swivel wheels and comfortable handles
• Some models can be folded with one hand	• The weight varies between different models and this won't necessarily be related to price – some of these supposedly lightweight pushchairs can be quite heavy to push
• Many models are relatively inexpensive compared with pram/pushchair combinations	
• Popular with toddlers as they feel less 'hemmed in'	• They don't have the suspension of many other pushchairs and the ride won't be as smooth
• Small, swivel wheels common to these pushchairs make them especially suitable for city and town streets	• They tend to lack decent-sized shopping storage space

 Large nursery chain stores, such as Babies 'R' Us, Mamas & Papas and Mothercare, will be able to advise you further. See pages 186–95 for Where to shop and also pages 204-11 for contact information for other retailers.

Pushchairs

The pushchair is the modern pram and comes in a variety of guises. The standard forward-facing pushchair has either a lie-back seat (ideally with a number of positions) or a reclining bucket seat, and is suitable for newborn babies and toddlers. A reversible seat unit that can be forward- or rear-facing has the option of giving your baby a reassuring view of you or, as they get older, the interest of looking around as they cruise along. Pushchairs fold down (check how easy this is) into a freestanding unit – unlike strollers, which usually need to be hung up or tend to end up sprawled across the floor.

" A forward-facing pushchair has a lie-back or reclining bucket seat and is suitable for newborn babies and toddlers. "

Suitable from birth?

Not all pushchairs recline enough to enable your baby to lie down flat so, when you are choosing a pushchair for a new baby, you need to make sure the seat can fully recline. New babies need the back support that only a fully reclining pushchair can give. The manufacturer should make it clear on the information accompanying the pushchair whether or not it is suitable for use from birth. If in doubt, ask the retailer.

Until your baby is about three or four months old you should still be careful about back support, and babies should not sit in a pushchair that doesn't have any sort of recline until they are six months or so (i.e. until they can sit up). Even at this age some recline facility is still better, if the pushchair is being used regularly, to enable your baby to sleep comfortably.

The pros and cons of forward-facing pushchairs

Pros	Cons
• Cheaper and lighter than more complicated pushchairs but more solid than a stroller	• Not as adaptable as combination pushchairs and travel systems
• Suitable from birth	
• Lie-back position makes them suitable for newborns, as well as older children	

Two- and three-in-ones

Pushchairs are also available in two-in-one (which adjusts from a lie-flat pram to a sit-up pushchair) and three-in-one (which also has a carrycot) combinations. If you like the idea of your new baby being in a pram but want a pushchair for when he or she is a bit older, the two-in-one or three-in-one combination could be a good choice.

Some three-in-one carrycots come with a mattress; some don't. If you want to use the carrycot for night-time sleeping, you need to check the mattress is appropriate – the manufacturer should specify if it is suitable for night-time use. If one doesn't come as part of the basic price, expect to pay extra for a night-time mattress.

Good as fold

A good folding mechanism can make a world of a difference to its ease of use. When you've got a baby or toddler in hand or on your hip, a simple one-handed movement is far preferable to struggling with clips, catches and buttons. If possible, try out your friends' models too and definitely test your purchase in the shop before you pay.

❝ If you buy a three-in-one with a carrycot, check the mattress is suitable for night-time use. ❞

The pros and cons of two- and three-in-one pushchairs

Pros	Cons
• Pram-style chassis will usually have better suspension than that of a standard buggy-style pushchair	• Their comparative bulk and weight can make these pushchairs feel cumbersome and they can be an obstruction at times
• Seats are normally both rearward- and forward-facing	• Large, fixed wheels are not as easy to manoeuvre as smaller, swivel wheels
• Many have fairly large, fixed wheels, which give a smoother ride, especially over rough ground	• You may find you use the pram option a lot but, by the time you move on to the pushchair, a lighter, more compact buggy-style pushchair may suit you more
• Lie-back or carrycot option is useful if you want to use a pushchair for daytime sleeps at home	• They are not a very portable option – although they fold, three-in-ones can still be heavy and can take up quite a lot of space
• Shopping-basket area is usually a reasonable size	

All-terrain pushchairs

These are typically three-wheelers with wide wheels fitted under a light, strong frame and a fabric, weatherproof seat, so they are great for bumpy terrain and country walks.

Three-wheelers are regarded by many as the most stylish pushchair you can buy. Originally designed to appeal to fitness enthusiasts and serious walkers who had started families but were still keen to pursue their training and interests, three-wheelers are now just as common a sight in the supermarket or the local park as on a hillside path. However, they are bulky compared with strollers, and can be difficult to steer and control over steps and kerbs, so they don't suit town life.

The idea is that they enable you to push your baby relatively smoothly over all kinds of terrain, from a beach to a muddy footpath to a pavement, with the tyres rather than your baby absorbing the bumps. If you prefer the idea of your new baby being in a completely flat, pram-style enclosure, you can get three-wheelers with a carrycot attachment.

Although many models fold easily, these aren't as compact when folded as many buggies; however, you can

! If you are planning to use your three-wheeler over rough ground, bear in mind that you shouldn't really do this until your baby is about six months old, as until this age babies' necks are not strong enough to take the strain of a bouncing head.

normally take the wheels off, which makes storage in the car boot easier. But they still aren't the quickest pushchair to get up and going once you get them out.

There is also a three-wheeler that can be converted into a double buggy by fitting a second seat in front of the first seat. If you like the idea of jogging with your pushchair, you can buy three-wheelers specially suited to this – you need to choose one with large wheels (with some models there is a choice of wheel size), a back axle that won't get in your way, a handbrake to control speed and a hand strap for extra security.

Travel systems

Travel systems allow you to move your baby with the mininum disturbance. They are large pushchairs that can be used with a car seat and/or a carrycot, so your baby can be moved from car to pushchair in one step. Not all these items are always part of the basic price, so be clear about what is included when you are buying. Both the car seat and the pushchair seat are suitable for use from birth – the pushchair reclines fully and

The pros and cons of pushchairs

All-terrain

Pros	Cons
• Suitable for those who are keen on the outdoor life, especially if you enjoy walking • Those with a front swivel wheel (not all have these) can be easier to handle than bulkier pram/pushchair combinations • Some models have an aluminium frame and are incredibly light – but these are at the pricier end of the market	• Their longer shape means they can be harder to manoeuvre in confined spaces than standard (forward-facing) pushchairs and can be unwieldy over steps and kerbs • Pneumatic tyres may make the ride smoother but they can also puncture

Travel systems

Pros	Cons
• Comfortable ride for your baby • Your baby can stay in the car seat to be moved from the car to the pushchair so there is less risk of waking him or her up • Buying the pushchair and car seat in one go means less time spent looking at all the different models of each • Useful if you also need to use public transport in the early days – you won't have to bundle your baby out of the pushchair to get on the bus	• Their comparative bulk and weight can make them feel cumbersome and they can be an obstruction • The attractions of a lighter, more compact buggy-style pushchair may mean you end up buying one of these later on • They are not a very portable option – although they fold, they can still be heavy, take up quite a lot of space and may not fit in smaller car boots • You need to be absolutely sure the car seat fits your car properly before you buy, as not all models fit every type of car • You must be wary of using the car seat as a pushchair seat too much: young babies' backs need to be well supported (see 'Suitable from birth?' box on page 142) • Bear in mind that you will need to buy another car seat within nine months or so, as the car seats to be used with these systems are only for young babies

the car seat is an infant type (for more on car seats see pages 114–22). Some car seats and carrycots slide on to the chassis, others clip on or are fastened with Velcro. Travel systems are usually four-wheeled and are heavy and quite bulky, even when folded. However, the convenience of the car seat compatibility is handy if you use the car a lot.

DOUBLE PUSHCHAIRS

If you are having twins or you have a young toddler and are expecting a baby, a double pushchair will probably be high up on your shopping list. The basic choice is between a side-by-side or a tandem style. Side-by-side pushchairs are usually suitable for twins from birth as well as for an older child and a baby. Tandem pushchairs tend to be suitable for a toddler and a baby, or two older babies, as usually only the back seat is

fully reclining. You can get two-in-one, three-in-one and three-wheeler versions of side-by-side pushchairs. There is less variety with tandem pushchairs.

With double pushchairs, more than with any other type, what is best for you depends on your own circumstances and preferences, and you may have to compromise on one feature at the expense of another – for example, if you want a side-by-side with reasonably roomy seats, you'll have to go for a wider model that won't fit as easily through many doorways.

Bear in mind that there are alternatives to double pushchairs – not so much for twins, but if you have a toddler and a baby, a sling and a light buggy, or a pushchair and some sort of toddler platform (see 'Pushchair accessories' on pages 150–2) may be a better choice for you.

BUYING SECOND-HAND

Pushchairs and prams are often bought second-hand or passed on between family or friends. If you will be using a second-hand pushchair, check for the following:

• Properly working brakes.
• Correctly aligned wheels.
• All folding parts operating smoothly.
• Two locking mechanisms working efficiently and safely (this is to ensure that the pushchair doesn't fold up or collapse while a child is in it).
• No rust or flaking paint or chrome.
• Fabric in reasonably good condition and not weakened by any tears.

The pros and cons of double pushchairs

Side-by-side pushchairs

Pros

- Tend to be more compact and portable than tandems
- Generally the most lightweight choice, although weight can vary hugely between models
- Fairly small, swivel wheels common to many side-by-side pushchairs are useful for manoeuvring around town
- Usually suitable for twins from birth as well as for a newborn and a toddler

Cons

- Can be more difficult to get through doorways than tandems
- Access to shopping basket may be tricky when seats are reclined
- On some models, the choice is between either fully upright or fully reclined seating, with no intermediate options – those with semi-recline as well are more flexible

Tandem pushchairs

Pros

- Compact shape width-wise means they are easier to manoeuvre through doorways
- Sturdier feel than many buggy-style, side-by-side pushchairs
- Tandem style makes it more difficult for an older child to harass a baby (although, in later months, the child seated in the back may enjoy pulling the hair of the child in front)

Cons

- Rear seat often has limited leg room so can be restrictive for an older baby
- Usually little head support in the front seat for a toddler who falls asleep
- Unless there are two hoods, some tandem models don't offer much weather protection for the child in the front seat
- More bulky and cumbersome to fold than side-by-side pushchairs
- Not as widely available as side-by-side pushchairs and less choice of styles
- Not easy to manoeuvre up and down kerbs

- Handles and frame with no unusual-looking bends or kinks.
- A five-point rather than a three-point harness; this conforms to current safety standards.

Manufacturers are usually willing to service and repair second-hand pushchairs and check that they conform to safety requirements so don't be afraid to ask if you think there's a problem.

Points to consider before buying: Pushchairs

There is an element of compromise involved in buying any kind of pushchair. You are unlikely to find one that meets all your needs perfectly because all types have their advantages and disadvantages and your requirements may change, too. However, by thinking carefully about factors such as where you live, how you plan to spend your days with your baby, whether you will be using public transport or how often you'll be climbing into the car, and even how soon you plan to have another baby, you can help ensure that you buy a pushchair that serves you well.

How heavy is it? If you need to lift the pushchair into the back of the car a lot, or up steps or stairs, weight is an important factor. A pram-style chassis (e.g. a two-in-one or three-in-one pushchair – see page 143) may be too cumbersome to get up the steps smoothly, and you will end up hauling your sleeping baby awkwardly up the steps. In such circumstances, you may well benefit from choosing a smaller, more lightweight option.

Decide where, ideally, you would like to store the pushchair and make sure the model you want is suitable. Don't fool yourself into thinking you'll be folding the pushchair every time you finish using it – realistically this is unlikely to happen, and you need to think of the pushchair in terms of its unfolded size, taking up space in the hallway. If you have a narrow hallway or other storage area, a bulky one may not be suitable for you. You need space for it and your shopping in the car boot.

Will you be using public transport regularly? If so, a lightweight, easy-folding pushchair or buggy that can be used from birth is what you need. Bear in mind that you will probably have the baby under one arm while you fold the pushchair, so you should buy one with a folding mechanism that you can operate with one hand or foot.

If your car boot is small, you'll need to check that the folded pushchair will fit into it. It is worth looking at the lighter, buggy-style options if you want to make lifting the pushchair in and out of the boot and folding and unfolding it as simple a task as possible.

A 'travel system' pushchair will incur less risk of waking up your baby, because you can attach the car seat, complete with sleeping baby, straight on to the pushchair chassis.

How long you will be using the pushchair for It's only worth paying for a two- or three-in-one if you are sure you will be using it over a couple of years. This is something hard to predict – but if you imagine yourself using the car a lot, visiting friends' houses, doing the shopping and fitting in strolls in the park, it's worth considering the advantages of a buggy-style pushchair. If you are planning to have more children, then using a lightweight buggy for the toddler and a sling for the baby, or a double buggy for both, will be the easiest way of getting around. Or it might pay to go for a better quality, durable and adaptable pushchair.

A sleeping vehicle If you expect that your baby will be using the pushchair instead of the cot for lengthy daytime naps, or you envisage whole afternoons in the park as a regular part of your routine with your new baby, a two-in-one or a three-in-one that comes with a carrycot and mattress is worth considering, as sleeping children should be placed on a firm horizontal base. You can use a sheet and blankets with the carrycot on a three-in-one, while, with a lie-back pushchair or a two-in-one, your baby is likely to be lying directly on the pushchair fabric. A traditional pram is also good for daytime naps although it is much less versatile in other respects.

Shopping-basket capacity varies widely between pushchair types. If you are likely to be using the pushchair to help you carry more shopping than a pint of milk and a loaf of bread, look at the size of the shopping basket (if there is one) with a couple of bags of shopping in mind (see box on page 151).

Buying more than one pushchair This can be the best option for many people as one type of pushchair may not suit all your requirements. You could, for example, have a two-in-one or three-in-one for daily use but also have a cheaper buggy for taking on holiday, for days out using the car or for using on public transport. You can buy a basic buggy, marketed as being suitable for a newborn baby, pretty cheaply. It won't be the most luxurious option for your baby but may be the most practical choice for you.

Comfort for both you and your baby Your baby is likely to be fine in almost anything. Whether you will be comfortable pushing it is another matter. Handle height is critical: if you or your partner are taller than average you don't want to be stooping to push your baby – check out the feel of the handle height in the shop or make sure the handles are adjustable. Handles with soft, rounded edges are kindest on the hands. Check that you don't scrape your shins on the rear axle as you walk and that the brake is easy to operate, whatever type of shoe you are wearing.

149

Pushchair accessories

Of course, you don't have to stop at buying the pushchair. Pushchair manufacturers and others have come up with a range of accessories designed for your or your baby's convenience or comfort. Bear in mind that some extras can add substantially to the cost of the basic pushchair.

TYPES OF ACCESSORY

One person's essential is another person's luxury. Ask your friends what they can't do without.

Rain covers

A decent rain cover will certainly protect your baby from the elements, but they can be a hassle to fold, unfold and fit in the first place, as well as being a moderately expensive extra. Some parents can't imagine being without one while others barely, if ever, use one. A few drops of rain aren't going to harm your baby, especially if he or she is protected by clothing and perhaps a pram or pushchair hood anyway. Older babies and toddlers may fight against having the rain cover put on and many parents give up altogether, especially if the rain doesn't seem particularly bad.

The most effective rain covers, should you choose to buy one, are 'all-in-one' and give your baby ample room to wave about or kick his or her legs without feeling claustrophobic. You can also buy showerproof covers quite cheaply –

these are elasticated pieces of showerproof fabric that you fit loosely over a pushchair, with a gap for your baby's head. They are very light so can be folded and kept in a bag for emergencies, and can be useful if you want some level of rain protection but don't want a full rain cover. Remember to take the rain cover off as soon as you get indoors otherwise your baby may overheat.

"The most effective rain covers are 'all-in-one' and give your baby plenty of room to move about. "

Toddler platforms

If you have a baby and an older child and you only want one pushchair in use at one time, a toddler platform can make your life easier. These are also known as 'buggy boards', a brand name of a main manufacturer. You fit the wheeled platform on to your pram or pushchair (you'll need to buy the right sort as they differ depending on what kind of pram or pushchair you have) and your toddler or pre-schooler can hop on when he or she doesn't want to walk. Some pushchairs are also made with an integrated platform. It is hard to predict before you buy how much use you will get out of one of these.

If your older child seems to enjoy walking and doesn't tend to moan about wanting to go in the pushchair, you can easily get by without one. Many parents who opt to buy one do find them useful, however, if only for a few months while their older child builds up his or her walking stamina. They can also be useful for getting from A to B quickly without having to chivvy a dawdling three-year-old to keep up. Almost certainly your pushchair has not been designed with an additional platform in mind so you will need to check it regularly for any signs of damage or excessive wear. Also check that there are no areas where your toddler could get his or her fingers or feet trapped.

❝A toddler platform can make life much easier, even if only for a few months while an older child builds up his or her walking stamina.❞

No hang-ups

The golden rule is not to hang shopping from the handles of a buggy or pushchair because if your toddler gets out, buggy and shopping end up overturned on the floor. More seriously it is also possible for a pushchair to 'up-end' with your baby in it if the bags are particularly heavy. Buggy weights are designed to be attached to the base of a buggy and provide enough ballast to hang a fair amount of shopping from the handles, reducing the risk of your buggy up-ending. Because they are attached to both front wheels the extra weight is evenly distributed so doesn't make a significant difference to the ease of pushing. The weights are easily removable for when you're not shopping, but you are then at risk of not remembering that you've taken them off. Where possible, carry all your shopping on the shopping tray supplied.

Changing bags

Many pushchair manufacturers produce changing bags to coordinate with the design of their pushchair fabrics. If you like the idea of everything matching, you may decide a coordinating bag is for you, but bear in mind that other changing bags could be worth a look and might be more suitable for your needs. For more on changing bags see pages 24–5.

Take a rain check

When you look at the price of a pushchair or buggy in the shop, check whether it includes a rain cover – some models do, some don't. You can only make meaningful price comparisons once you know what is included in the display price.

Sun canopies and parasols

These are widely available and can help to shade your baby on sunny days – but they are often ineffective on their own simply because the sun and the pushchair will be changing positions as you walk and as the day goes on. Parasols, in particular, need to be regularly adjusted, can be fiddly and may end up being simply annoying. To be sure of sun protection when using a parasol or canopy, check that exposed areas of your baby's skin are protected by clothing and/or covered with a high-protection children's sun cream and that he or she is wearing a sun hat (see pages 135–8).

Footmuffs

Retailers and manufacturers often recommend you buy one of these to go with your new pushchair, if one isn't already included. It is a sort of 'bottom-half' sleeping bag, which helps keep your baby warm and offers some protection against the elements. Footmuffs are not essential and many parents are happy to keep their baby warm with blankets, but they can make keeping your baby snug a bit easier. Some foot muffs convert to pram quilts and liners.

Head support cushions

These give young babies extra support and comfort in pushchairs, car seats and bouncing chairs.

Insect and cat nets

If you plan to have your baby napping in the pram in the garden during the summer, insect and cat nets, which fit over the whole body of the pram, can give you a bit more peace of mind.

Pushchair toys

There is a wide range of toys available that you can attach to the pushchair so your baby can play without the toy falling out of reach. These range from rattles and soft toys to relatively elaborate play devices that fit across the pushchair so your baby can press and tweak all manner of buttons and knobs. Bear in mind that, whatever the toy, the more your baby sees it, the less novel it will be, so if you can, try to change pushchair toys fairly regularly.

From baby to toddler

Your baby's emotional and practical needs change enormously from now on. This chapter starts with a thorough look at the crucial topic of safety in the home and what you can do or buy to ensure it. It also offers guidance on what to look for in play equipment for young children, and what products can help you through the delights of toilet training and – perhaps less stressfully – bathtime.

6

Safety

Babies are vulnerable creatures, especially in the bathroom where the twin dangers of water and heat are often combined. As your baby grows, new safety concerns arise.

Toddlers will inevitably fall and trip in their uncoordinated efforts to explore. They don't understand the concept of danger, so may ignore or forget your warnings about what they should or shouldn't do. Each year, about 600,000 children aged under five are injured in the home badly enough to go to hospital. You can help prevent your child from joining these statistics by being vigilant, and with the help of some of the products outlined opposite and over the following pages.

It is also fair to say that most safety gadgets present some level of inconvenience to adults, so even if you have them you may be tempted not to use them all the time. Neither are they effective for all age groups – overcoming them depends on the skills level that children have reached, and if there are older children in the house you have to try to make sure they don't leave cupboards, gates and doors open. So even with the extra protection afforded by these products, you still need to be vigilant.

❝No home is hazardproof but here are some ways that you can help yourself and your young children.❞

 Children may be at additional risk in other people's homes, particularly those of grandparents where any childproofing has long since ceased to be an issue.

 The Child Accident Prevention Trust (CAPT), a charity that educates and campaigns on safety issues relating to children, has a range of free leaflets on different aspects of baby and child safety. You can send off for them or download a selection of safety fact sheets from its website: www.capt.org.uk.

HAZARDS IN AND AROUND THE HOME

No home is childproof. Here, some of the most common hazards in your home (and, of course, those of anyone you visit or any holiday accommodation you go to) are explained.

Poisoning

Many chemicals such as bleach and medicines come with childproof tops. However, these are often difficult to undo and there is a temptation not to replace the top in its safe position – and some older people find it difficult to open childproof containers and so leave them open. Care must therefore be taken to keep these products away from children. You can keep the medicines in a lockable cabinet (see page 163), the household chemicals in an inaccessible or lockable cupboard and garden chemicals locked away in a shed or the garage. However, if you are visiting other people, their potentially dangerous substances may not be safely out of reach.

> **!** If grandparents or other older visitors are staying with you, keep an eye open to make sure that they don't leave any medication with the top undone, something they might do out of habit.

Choking

Choking is a serious hazard to young children. Even if a small object passes from the child's mouth into the child's stomach, there is a risk of toxic contamination or internal blockages. Toys often carry a warning indicating that they are not suitable for children under three years of age because of small parts that children can place in their mouths. There are many other small objects around the home that need to be kept out of the reach of babies and toddlers. For example, all UK coins are small enough to choke a child.

> **"** Take care to keep such chemicals as bleach and medicines out of the reach of children. **"**

Getting trapped

If a child traps a knee between bars, such as those on stairs and playpens, he or she will be distressed, but there shouldn't be any serious injury. If, however, they slip feet-first through a gap that is too small for the head to pass through, they could be trapped or even strangled. Check your stairs and landing to see if there are any gaps where a child could slip through feet-first.

Entanglement

A cord wrapped around a child's neck can strangle. Position cots so that the child cannot reach a curtain or blind cord. Ensure that cords or ties on homemade clothes or knitwear are less than 20cm (8in) long, and that bags for stowing toys or clothes have an opening of less than 36cm (14in) so that they cannot pass over the child's head, especially if they have a drawstring. Never tie a child's dummy on to a ribbon round its neck and if your child wears a necklace or chain, remember that this could get snagged on a protrusion.

Suffocation

A thin piece of plastic covering the child's nose and mouth can mould itself to the child's face and block the air supply to the lungs. Plastic bags from the supermarket will almost certainly have holes in them for ventilation but many others do not. For safety, keep all plastic bags and plastic packaging out of the reach of children. Never let your child play with any form of plastic packaging or wrapping material and don't attach transfers to his or her cot as they can come off and become a choking hazard.

Glass

Any glass objects can present a hazard so keep these out of reach (see opposite for safety glass and safety film). Never let a child play on glass-topped tables.

> **!** If you secure your windows with a lock and key, make sure that anyone baby sitting knows where the key is in an emergency.

Greenhouses and cold frames are a hazard in the garden. If you have either, make sure it has safety glass or plastic sheets, but you are going to need to be careful when in other people's gardens.

Drowning

A child can drown within seconds in a very small quantity of water, so never leave yours alone where there is access to open water. The bath is an obvious danger area but so are ponds and paddling pools, even if they have been emptied, as they fill with rainwater. Do not leave pails with water within reach of a child, and put nappies to soak in a pail with a secure lid.

❝ Never leave your child alone where there is access to open water – a child can drown within seconds in a very small quantity. ❞

LIVING ROOM

Most accidents happen in the living room, mainly because this is where most family activity takes place. Devices to consider include the following.

Fireguard

If you have any sort of fire, a fireguard is a must. It needs to be full size and hooked to the wall for maximum safety.

A proper fireguard should also have a top that prevents items from being thrown into the fire – a curved top is best because this is also a deterrent against placing objects on it. A simple spark guard or fire screen (a smaller guard designed to offer protection against sparks from an open fire, which is positioned much closer to the fire, with minimal 'overhead' protection and not secured to the wall) is not sufficient to protect your child. Fireguards are widely available from nursery stores and catalogues (see page 204–11).

Radiator guards

These prevent your child burning him- or herself on a hot radiator. Try one of the larger DIY stores.

Corner guards

These are plastic corner covers to help protect babies and toddlers from bumps against low tables and shelves.

Door slam stoppers

These prevent doors from shutting on small fingers and also stop children from shutting themselves in a room. Some types of stopper prevent fingers from getting trapped in one side of the door but not the other – for example, the hinge side might be protected but the door can still be closed.

If you want maximum protection, choose a stopper designed to protect both sides. Alternatively, use a door stop to prevent the door from moving at all. You can also buy stoppers designed for sliding patio doors.

Glass safety film

If you are fitting new glass in your home (for example, glass doors to your patio), you must use safety glass. The characteristics of safety glass depend on the type – for example, toughened glass breaks into blunt shapes rather than sharp shards, while laminated glass will 'craze' but won't actually crack. If you have existing doors that aren't made of safety glass, you can cover the glass with safety film, which will contain any jagged shards should the glass break. You can also use this for glass-topped tables.

Socket covers

Electricity isn't a major contributor to child accident statistics, but many parents feel reassured by having socket covers in place. Choose plain, simple ones – you want to make the socket area boring rather than inviting. A better option than buying covers for every socket is to protect your house's wiring with a residual current device (RCD). This is basically an electricity 'cut-out' device, which protects against electrocution by automatically cutting the electricity supply within a fraction of a second if it detects a fault or an unusual surge.

❝ Choose plain and simple socket covers so they look as uninteresting as possible. ❞

157

Video and DVD locks

Little fingers just can't seem to stay away from the video slot. A simple video lock covers the slot so your child can't shove fingers or small objects in. This is useful as a video-damage prevention device as much as a mechanism to prevent your child's fingers getting trapped. A DVD lock prevents accidental operation of the machine.

Playpen

If you need to leave a crawling baby or young toddler alone in a room for a short while, perhaps to answer the door or telephone, a playpen can be a useful 'security zone' in which to place him or her.

Toy box

Although not a safety device as such, it is a good idea to have a box in your living room or wherever your child's toys tend to accumulate. Toys left on the floor are a tripping hazard, and a handy box for you to throw everything in when you get the chance is a good preventive measure. Make sure you get one with a slow-closing hinge so that little fingers can't get bruised by a slamming lid.

 Hot drinks on low tables or the arms of chairs can cause serious burns to babies and toddlers. Bear in mind that a cup of tea or coffee can be hot enough to burn for as long as 20 minutes after it has been made.

❝The slot in the video or DVD player is very tempting for young fingers. Simple locks are available and will prevent your child's fingers becoming trapped.❞

Information on playpens is given on pages 177-8 and for gates and barriers, see page 162.

KITCHEN

The kitchen is full of potential dangers. Obvious ones are burns and scalds from kettles, pans and cookers; swallowing or touching dangerous fluids; or injury from kitchen implements. Gadgets to prevent these accidents include the following.

Cupboard and drawer catches

These are designed to allow a cupboard or drawer to be opened only a few centimetres unless an adult releases the catch. Children will eventually learn how to operate them, but in the meantime they can provide a degree of reassurance.

Hob guard

These can help prevent young children reaching up to hot surfaces or pulling on cooking pot handles. However, they aren't necessarily a good idea. Some guards can get hot enough to cause burns themselves, and some have bars that children's fingers can get through. Also, you need to lift a pan over a hob guard, which could in itself cause an accident.

Gate or barrier

The best way of preventing your child from the dangers of the kitchen is to try to keep him or her out of there as much as possible. A gate or barrier is the best way of doing this, as your child can still watch you when you are in the kitchen but will be out of harm's way. Otherwise a playpen will keep them safe, assuming you have space for it.

Fridge guard/lock

This is a simple catch that you attach to the side of the fridge. The fridge surface to which you attach it needs to be clean and grease-free, otherwise the guard can be easily pulled off.

Curly flex

A curly flex on a kettle can help prevent your child from pulling on the appliance and pouring boiling water over him- or herself.

(*Continued on page 162*)

> **There are plenty of gadgets designed for the kitchen, which is a place that is full of potential dangers.**

When cooking, use the back burners or hotplates whenever possible, and turn the pan handles towards the back. Keep the kettle and its flex to the back of the work surface, out of children's reach at all times. Water is still hot enough to scald for at least 20 minutes after boiling.

First aid

You can buy ready-stocked first-aid kits from many stores, but if you want to be sure you have everything you might need, it's worth putting together your own kit. All the items listed below should be available to buy separately from a well-stocked chemist. Keep your kit in a secure box out of your child's reach and check the contents regularly in case anything needs to be replaced. Make sure that other adults who may look after your child at your home know where your first-aid box is. A well-stocked first-aid kit should contain:

✓ Infant/child thermometer (preferably digital and not one containing mercury as this can be a hazard if damaged)

✓ Children's and infants' liquid pain reliever

✓ An oral syringe or calibrated cup or spoon for administering medicines to infants and children

✓ 1 small roller bandage

✓ 1 large roller bandage

✓ 1 small conforming bandage (these shape themselves to the body contours)

✓ Scissors

✓ Pack of gauze swabs

✓ 2 triangular bandages (can be used as slings)

✓ Safety pins in a variety of sizes (for securing dressings)

✓ Hypoallergenic tape (for securing dressings)

✓ 2 sterile pads

✓ Waterproof plasters

✓ 1 finger bandage and applicator

✓ Tweezers

✓ 1 sterile dressing with bandage

✓ Vinyl gloves

✓ Mild liquid soap (most antibacterial and deodorant soaps are too strong for babies' sensitive skin)

✓ Calamine cream

✓ Antibacterial cream

✓ Sting reliever spray

✓ Eyewash solution

> **Put together your own first-aid kit to ensure that you have all possible eventualities covered.**

Various household items can also be used successfully in a first-aid emergency – for burns in particular. For example:

✔ A clean sheet or pillowcase can make an effective loose protective covering for burns.

✔ Plastic kitchen film can be used to dress burns.

✔ A clean plastic bag can be secured around a burned hand or foot.

> **To deal with a burn you need a clean sheet or pillowcase, plastic kitchen film or a clean plastic bag.**

 Keep your first-aid items in a waterproof container large enough for the contents to be arranged so that items can be found quickly. A plastic container with a closely fitting lid would be suitable. It's a good idea to label it so that it can be easily recognised by anybody. Standard labelling for a first-aid box is a green background with a white cross.

> **Store your first-aid items in a plastic container with a closely fitting lid and add a label so it can be easily recognised by anybody.**

STAIRS, HALLWAY AND LANDING

Crawling babies and toddlers can sustain serious injuries falling down the stairs. It is worth making the stairs inaccessible to them until they are steady on their feet and more aware of the dangers. There are a couple of devices you can use to protect them.

Barriers and gates

These are usually meant only for children up to about two years old (three- and four-year-olds will probably be capable of opening them). Ideally you need two barriers or gates – one at the top of the stairs and one at the bottom. Many gates have a low bar across the bottom, which makes them more stable. However, adults could trip over this bar when they are going through the gate at the top of the stairs, so you need to be extra careful with these (although you may be able to buy an anti-trip attachment). Rigid, fixed barriers are more awkward to negotiate than gates if you need to move around the house in a hurry. You can also buy fabric barriers that roll back when not in use so they are less obtrusive.

There are portable barriers that fit across openings using pressure to secure them into position. These are particularly useful when on holiday or visiting grandparents. Some gates are sold claiming that they are automatic, that is, they will close behind you. However, if you buy one of these, check that it is truly automatic, closing from whatever the angle you leave it at, as some will only close and latch if they have been

opened quite wide. Also, you should not assume that the gate will shut each and every time: you need to check that it has shut behind you and you also need to be sure that your child is not in the way as it closes.

Whether you choose a barrier or a gate, ideally you should be able to open it with one hand as you may be carrying a child. If you are fitting the barrier or gate at the bottom of the stairs, do not fit it on the floor but on the first step: this will prevent your child getting a foothold part-way up the barrier. Sometimes this isn't possible, so place the barrier on the front of the first available step. Also, if the design of your staircase enables you to, place the barrier or gate back from the top step.

Smoke alarm

This is an essential safety device. You should have these in your house anyway, but having children often galvanises people into installing smoke alarms if they haven't done so before. If you live in a flat or bungalow, one alarm should be

> **!** Barriers and gates will not be effective if they are badly fitted or if the surfaces to which you attach them aren't sound, so check for wobbly banisters and suspect plaster that could give way under pressure.

enough in the hallway. If your home has more than one floor, however, put one alarm at the bottom of the stairs and one on each upstairs landing. Test the alarms monthly, at least, to make sure they are operating correctly and replace the batteries every year.

❝ The main dangers to children in a bathroom are drowning in the bath water and poisoning from medicines and toxic cleaners that haven't been safely stored. ❞

> Never leave a baby or a young child alone in or near a bath, even for a moment. Accidents can happen in a few seconds and a baby can drown in 2.5cm (1in) of water.

BATHROOM

The key dangers to children in a bathroom are drowning in the bath water and poisoning from medicines and toxic cleaners that haven't been safely stored away. Other risks include slipping on wet surfaces and scalding from hot water. Devices to consider include the following.

Medicine cabinet

One that you can lock is best, even if you think the cabinet is out of your child's reach. Before too long he or she will be moving chairs or clothes baskets around to use as a platform to stand on. Consider having this cabinet in a room where you spend much of your time, such as the kitchen.

Thermostatic mixing valve (TMV)

TMVs are control devices that mix hot water from your boiler with your cold-water supply in such a way that the water coming out of your tap never exceeds a preset temperature. They are now compulsory in new developments in Scotland and similar legislation is earmarked for the rest of the UK. Each TMV should dramatically reduce the number of children who are scalded by bath water every year (75 per cent of severe scalds involve the under-fives). TMVs are not generally available from

If you are anxious about the temperature of your baby's bath, you can buy a bath thermometer and other warning devices. Information on this is given on page 35.

From baby to toddler

DIY stores and can only be bought from plumbing or building suppliers. The manufacturers also recommend that only a plumber should fit them.

Non-slip bath mat

Young children see the bath as a playground and will want to stand up and mess around, particularly if there is more than one of them in the bath. A simple bath mat will prevent your child from slipping on the base of the bath.

Toilet seat lock

This will prevent your child from opening the toilet lid and putting his or her hands inside the toilet.

Toilet steps and adaptors

These can help children feel more secure and prevent them from falling off when they are learning to use the toilet.

NURSERY

Falling out of an upstairs window is the most serious hazard presented by any upstairs room. As well as taking precautions against this, you may want to consider fitting cupboard locks or door slam stoppers in the nursery if trapped fingers are a worry. Other safety products include the following.

Baby monitors

These shouldn't be regarded as a safety device. They are more for convenience, so you can hear your child crying if you are in another part of the house or in the garden. But they can alert you to potential hazards such as your child climbing out of the cot or bed. For more on baby monitors (see pages 36–41).

Window locks

Most windows without a lock are potentially hazardous to a small child, but upstairs windows in the nursery or

> **!** If you have window locks with a key, make sure that anyone who is looking after your child knows where the key is in case there is an emergency.

"Upstairs windows are especially potentially hazardous to a small child, so ensure they are safely locked."

 For more information on non-slip bath mats, see page 184; for learning to use the toilet, see pages 179-82; for cupboard locks, see page 159 and for baby monitors, see pages 36-41.

another bedroom are particularly worth making child-resistant. Some lock with a separate key (so you have to keep it somewhere accessible to you but not to your child); others are keyless and have a mechanism that requires you to do two actions at once (which should foil a small child). All allow the window to open a couple of centimetres when they're in use.

Bed guard

This can help prevent your child from falling out of bed until he or she is used to being in a bed rather than a cot. You can choose from grid-like styles or soft mesh styles with a rigid edge. As long as you have one side of the bed against the wall, you'll only need one guard. Bear in mind that lots of children take to a bed very easily and rarely, if ever, fall out and that, even if they do, a bump and a bit of a shock is all they're likely to get. Make sure that the bed is placed as close to the wall as possible so that your child can't slip down between the bed and the wall and get trapped.

 Keep furniture, including beds, away from windows, so that young children won't be able to climb on to them to get to the window.

Toys

Finding the right toys for your child is a hit-and-miss affair. No matter how much research you put into it, how many shops or catalogues you scour or other parents you get advice from, you will end up with some toys that your child loves and others that just gather dust.

Depending on your child's ability to concentrate, even the popular toys may provide only a short period of entertainment before he or she moves on to something else – and every parent has witnessed (or will do) their child casting a new toy aside only to play with the box it came in or the label attached!

You have more chance of getting it right at least some of the time if you familiarise yourself with the various stages of your child's development. Then toys can be bought to fit in with the abilities and interests of your baby as he or she grows up, and you can usefully brief present-givers. Arguably, certainly during the first year, you don't really need to buy any manufactured toys at all – you're bound to be given some and you're likely to find everything else you need to stimulate your baby around the house (see page 169). On the other hand, there is a certain pleasure in choosing and buying toys for your baby so, if you are going to do it anyway, it's worth following the guidelines given here.

MATCHING TOYS TO YOUR BABY'S DEVELOPMENT

Choose toys appropriate to your baby's age. Although all babies are different and some will react badly to or take little notice of a toy that another may like, the list below should help you make some good choices. Some toys will be multi-activity so you won't necessarily have to buy a separate toy for each characteristic. Remember, too, that a toy your baby may dislike one week may prove fascinating if reintroduced a couple of weeks later, so don't cast aside rejected toys straightaway. Bear in mind that you don't have to have the latest 'all-singing, all-dancing' electronic baby toys – the classics (such as stacking towers, balls and building blocks) have long remained popular for good reason.

Birth to three months

Babies' hearing is better developed than their eyesight in the early weeks, and they will respond to noise and music. Your baby will first notice light and contrasting colours, particularly black against white, then move on to colourful shapes and clearly defined patterns as well as moving objects. He or she will learn to focus more as time goes on. Babies can open and close their hands from birth, then start to notice their fingers and, after about two or three months, begin to recognise that certain things happen when they move their hands. At this stage, they will start reaching out for objects. Toys to consider for your baby include:

- **Mobiles,** particularly musical ones and those with patterns or objects that face your baby when he or she is lying in the cot.
- **Toys with in-built mirrors.** Your baby won't be able to recognise him- or herself until nearly two years old, but will be fascinated by the reflections in the mirror.
- **Brightly coloured, noisy rattles.**
- **Toys with high-contrast patterns,** such as simple faces.

Three to six months

By this age, babies are becoming better at reaching out for, grasping and holding objects, and may even be able to move them from one hand to the other. Their hands and the things they can hold will be explored with lips and tongue. They can sit with some support, can follow a moving object well and will look around for the source of sounds. Toys to consider include:

- Baby gym or activity arch with a good selection of toy attachments to bash and swipe at.
- Baby 'nest', a textile-covered inflatable ring or play mat with different textures, flaps and squeaks.
- Soft toys with interesting textures and chewable attachments (but see 'Phthalates', page 184).
- Easy-to-grip plastic balls with different sounds inside.

Six to nine months

By now, babies' coordination can have developed enough for them to be able to strike an object (such as a drum) with some control, and they will enjoy hitting one object against another. Your baby will be learning that he or she is the one in control of some activities and can choose when to start and when to stop. Babies of this age will also start to explore

---

Focal point

A new baby's eyes can only focus on near objects, so hold your face – and new toys – about 30cm (12in) from his or hers.

 For further information, go to www.literacytrust.org.uk/talktoyourbaby/play.html, which is concerned with the importance of play in your child's development.

objects properly with their hands and fingers as well as with their mouths. Toys to consider include:

- Musical instrument toys, especially drums.
- Toys that 'react' if you press a button or push a lever.
- Toys with flaps or lids that can be opened and closed.

Nine to twelve months

Babies are more mobile now – they are pulling themselves up, crawling or beginning to walk. They may be starting to get interested in playthings that help with their mobility and toys that they can move along themselves. Their fingers are more dextrous and they can manipulate smaller objects than they could before. Your baby will know that if a toy has fallen, it will be somewhere on the floor, and he or she will be interested in finding 'hidden' objects. Toys to consider include:

- Simple push-along toys, such as chunky, easy-to-hold vehicles, if your baby is mobile.
- Balls.
- Push-along baby walker.
- Toys your baby can play with in the bath, including items such as plastic cups as well as manufactured toys designed for the bath.

12 to 18 months

Babies of this age may start to put bits of objects together or take them apart and will find pleasure in knocking things down. They can put shapes into holes, their limbs are much more coordinated and they will be 'getting into everything'. They can point at objects when asked. Toys to consider include:

- Shape sorters.
- Stacking towers.
- Simple sit-on riding toys.
- Wooden puzzles with shaped pieces to match with shapes on the board.
- Stiff board books, the pages of which your baby can turn by him- or herself.

Books

It's never too early to start looking at books with your baby. Even when too young to understand what you are saying, he or she will enjoy hearing your voice. The best first books to show your baby are those with simple pictures of familiar objects in bold, bright colours, and with no or minimal text. Once your baby is seven to nine months, he or she may start to appreciate hearing very simple stories.

 See the useful addresses on pages 204-11 for contact details for a wide range of shops who sell toys for children of all ages.

18 to 24 months

By this stage, toddlers are more proficient at building and sorting. They may show an interest in 'make-believe' games involving dolls, animals and vehicles. Your child will be keen on playing outside on simple playground equipment, and he or she may also start to want to make things. Toys to consider include:

- Dolls and their paraphernalia, such as mini buggies and bottles.
- Child-sized ride-along cars and trucks.
- A first train set.
- Building blocks.
- Play dough.
- Matching games.
- 'Discovery' box. Set aside a box in which to put all manner of household items that are safe for your baby to play with. Make sure there are no small removable parts (see 'Play safe' box, page 171). You could include items such as textile off-cuts, plastic cups and spoons to bang together, an old TV remote control (but remove the batteries). Change the items regularly so your baby or toddler knows that his or her box might often contain something new.

❝ It's never too early to start looking at books with your baby. Even if he or she doesn't understand what you are saying, your voice will be soothing. ❞

 You can use all manner of everyday household items to keep your baby amused. However, if you do make your own, you must make sure that they are safe. Any small parts must be firmly attached. Making a cuddly animal is a lovely idea, but the stitching or sticking will need to be sound so that your baby can't get hold of the stuffing.

TOY SAFETY

Most toys on the market today are carefully made and safe to play with. Manufacturers have to conform to strict Europe-wide safety standards. But toys can still be hazardous if you don't take care over what you give your child.

Check you are happy with the safety of any toys you buy or are given, and always keep an eye out for damage that could render them dangerous. Follow these guidelines:

- **To be quite sure of safety,** get your toys from a retailer with a good reputation for toys or buy only recognised brand names.
- **Follow the age recommendations** on the packaging – they are there for a reason. Most are intended to give you a guide to the toy's 'fun factor' suitability for children of specific ages,

but any warning stating that a toy is unsuitable for children under three, for example, must be taken seriously as this indicates that the toy may be unsafe for younger children because of small parts.

- Look for the 'Lion mark' – this is a mark of quality and safety used by manufacturers who are members of the British Toy and Hobby Association – the main toy trade association in the UK.

- **!** Use a toy box – toys lying on the floor are a serious tripping hazard.
- Throw away broken or partially broken toys.
- Keep batteries out of the reach of children and don't mix them – new batteries can make the older ones very hot.

! The 'CE' mark is another symbol you may see on toy packaging – this is a mandatory mark that must appear on toys sold within the EU and shows that toys should conform to EU laws and can be sold throughout the EU (although the mark does not mean the toy has been independently tested for safety). Be wary of products that are 'toy-like' but don't have this mark (novelties, for example) – they may not be safe for young children to play with.

- Take special care buying second-hand toys and check for broken or small, loose parts (see pages 197–9).
- Once you have bought a toy, dispose of the packaging carefully – although fascinating to young children, it could harbour unseen hazards such as staples or sharp wire. If you let your child play with the packaging, inspect it carefully first.

 The 'CE' and Lion marks are but two of several symbols you will come across on equipment and games. See pages 187 for an explanation as to what each one means.

Play safe

- Remove bulky toys from the cot or playpen as soon as your child can stand, as they can provide a foothold for climbing out.
- Make sure any toys attached to the cot are on a very short piece of string, no longer than 20cm (8in), otherwise they could be a strangulation risk.
- Keep very furry soft toys away from your baby – the fur could be a choking hazard. (The official guidance relating to 'long fibres' is that these toys shouldn't be played with by children under 18 months, and wording to this effect should appear on the label.

Many manufacturers, however, use the more general recommendation of 'not for children under three' – see next point.)

- Check that the eyes, noses, bells and other trinkets on soft toys are firmly attached and remove any ribbons. Objects that are small enough for babies to put in their mouths are regarded as a choking risk until the age of about three, when children have less need to explore things with their mouths.
- Keep toys for older children separate from those for younger children.

❝ Keep very furry soft toys away from your baby and check that the eyes, noses, bells and other trinkets on all soft toys are firmly attached. ❞

Baby bouncers

Many babies adore these – and so do the watching adults. Your baby sits in a special seat that is attached to a long elasticated strip, the top of which is clamped to the doorframe, pushes against the floor with his or her feet, and bounces up and down.

Baby bouncers can be used from about four months of age – as soon as your baby can support his or her head. The bouncing sensation can delight babies (and be hilarious to watch) and this will probably be the first time your baby has felt the thrill of being able to move fast using his or her own leg muscles. However, even babies who love these bouncers may tire of them after ten minutes or so, and you should keep sessions fairly brief – 15 minutes is fine; 30 minutes the absolute limit. Not all babies like bouncing, so it may be worth borrowing a bouncer to try out before you buy.

&&Not all babies like bouncing so you might want to borrow a bouncer to try out before you go ahead and buy one.

TYPES OF BOUNCER

There are two types of baby bouncer – the main difference being between a simple, fabric seat like a pair of trousers or a seat with a moulded plastic surround, sometimes in the shape of a cartoon character or animal. Both types have their advantages and disadvantages (see opposite).

Whichever type of seat you choose, you need to make sure your doorframes and doorways are suitable for a bouncer. The frame must be sturdy and solid as it will need to take the weight of your baby. It should also be perfectly straight and the gap between the frame and the wall should be wide enough for the clamp to fit on to it properly. Most doorframes are fine but it is worth double-checking before you buy. Narrow doorways are not particularly suitable for bouncer use because your baby will bounce sideways as well as up and down, so he or she could knock against the frame. You will also need to ensure that the bouncer does not slide sideways as the baby is using it.

The pros and cons of bouncers

Plastic-seat bouncers

Pros	Cons
• Provides protection against bumps on the doorframe • Wipes clean	• Can be more constricting than the fabric type (and therefore possibly less fun for your baby) • Takes up space both to use and to store • Can be dangerous if an older child joins the baby for bouncing

Fabric-seat bouncers

Pros	Cons
• Smaller seat gives a bit more freedom for your baby to move and flail arms about. • Lightweight and easy to fold and store • Less expensive than plastic-seat type	• Provides less protection against knocks and may make your baby feel more vulnerable

Baby walkers

A baby walker is basically a seat (usually plus a table) within a wheeled frame. Your baby can sit in the walker and trundle about by pushing along with his or her feet.

Despite the name, baby walkers are not designed to help a baby learn to walk – more to provide them with mobility and entertainment at a time when they might be starting to get frustrated at their inability to get about.

Many parents swear by the usefulness of baby walkers, especially for babies with lots of 'get up and go', but the products have also had a bad press. Safety experts would prefer that parents avoided baby walkers altogether. The main problem with baby walkers was instability when encountering an uneven surface, such as the edge of a carpet or a doorstep, and this, often combined with the fair speed at which some babies can 'drive' them, could make them prone to tipping over. As well as overturning on to the floor, walkers and their occupants could fall down stairs, roll against fires and heaters, and tip into swimming pools.

However, new safety standards require walkers to have anti-tipping devices and as a result move at a slower speed. The latest walkers have been designed so that if they get their wheels over a top step they should halt and then not tip over. Walkers can also take you by surprise because they can suddenly move away from you, particularly in a backwards direction, and they also enable your baby to reach for things that you may not be prepared for, such as items on a low shelf or the corner of a table cloth, dragging the contents on to the floor.

So if walkers are so widely regarded as dangerous, why would anyone want to buy one? The simple answer is that babies can have a lot of fun in them and they can considerably broaden the horizons of those who may have been getting frustrated with the same old routine. The danger really arises when parents or carers do not watch their charges while they are in the walker – the babies most likely to be hurt in walker accidents are those who are left in them while their parents' attention is elsewhere, even for a short time.

> **!** Baby walkers are often passed on from one parent to another. Avoid using the older-style types described here as they are a safety hazard.

The pros and cons of baby walkers

Pros	Cons
• Babies usually have fun using baby walkers • They fold flat enough for you to store under a bed when not in use	• The potential hazards with the use of baby walkers are a real concern, so if you are planning to use one you do need to be vigilant • Their use may be limited to a fairly short developmental period – maybe only a few weeks – between sitting and crawling or walking, so you may decide the expense and possibly the extra anxiety, isn't worth it • There may be a temptation, if your baby really enjoys using the walker, to keep him or her in it for too long; but use should be limited to no more than 30 minutes at a time as your baby still needs the full range of movement at this stage of development

From baby to toddler

WALKER SAFETY

Here's how to let your child enjoy a walker safely.

• Only buy (or use, if someone is passing one on to you) a baby walker that complies with BS EN 1273:2005: the date is important (the last four digits are the year the standard was approved, in this case, 2005) because that's when more stringent safety requirements were imposed.
• Never leave your baby unattended in a walker.
• Never let your baby use the walker near steps, stairs or thresholds.

• If possible, confine use of the walker to one room at a time, keeping doors shut.
• Check that surfaces are flat and free of objects that may cause tipping over.
• Be extra vigilant if allowing your baby to use the walker in the garden, especially as the surface – on a patio, for example – may be uneven.
• Check that both your baby's feet touch the floor – the seat height should be adjustable for this purpose.
• Never carry the walker with your baby in it.
• Avoid use near fires or stoves – and radiators, if possible.

175

- **Always use the crotch strap** that is supplied with the walker, ensuring that your baby has a leg on each side of it.
- **Stop using the walker** when your baby reaches the maximum weight recommended by the manufacturer.
- **Walkers are not suitable** for babies who cannot support their heads or who are already accomplished walkers.
- **Limit use** to a maximum of 30 minutes at a time.
- **Remember that** your child will move much more quickly when in the walker, particularly in a reverse direction, than when crawling.

PLAY STATION

If you don't like the idea of a baby walker but would like your baby to have a new and potentially exciting play place in your home, you could think about a stationary baby 'play station' or 'static exerciser' instead.

These have a similar design to baby walkers but don't have wheels – instead your baby sits and swivels around to enjoy all it has to offer. Although a play station doesn't provide the same experience as a baby walker, the fun for your baby comes from pushing with his or her legs to spin the seating area around and rock to and fro.

The pros and cons of play stations

Pros	Cons
• Babies will have fun in this play space • Safe alternative to a baby walker	• Their use may be limited to a fairly short developmental period, so you may decide the expense isn't worth it • The novelty may wear off quickly

Playpens

A playpen can be a safe and compact play area for your crawling baby and provides a convenient security zone so that, if you have to nip out of the living room briefly, you know that he or she can't get into any trouble in your absence.

Some babies may also like the feeling of the playpen being 'their' place to play, nap or simply watch your activities. On the downside, playpens take up a lot of space and not all babies take well to being hemmed in – you could find that you have spent your money on a pricey, space-occupying storage box into which you put all manner of baby-related bits and pieces but not a baby.

If you decide to buy a playpen, do it before your baby is moving around so that you can get him or her familiar with it – there is then a better chance of it being a hit rather than a flop later on. For the same reason, if you have the space, go for a pen with a reasonably large floor area.

TYPES OF PLAYPEN

Traditional wooden playpens have been joined in the market by brightly coloured plastic pens, playpens with a folding metal structure surrounded by mesh and travel cots that double up as playpens (see pages 49–51 for information on travel cots).

> **!** Multifunctional products that double-up as barriers to doors and stairs are sometimes referred to as playpens or play yards. These products do not normally have a base attached to the side barriers so that it is fairly easy for your baby or older siblings to move them around. They are therefore not as safe as a traditional style playpen.

Clean pad

A removable floor pad or mattress is preferable to one that is fixed because it makes cleaning much easier.

The pros and cons of playpens

Wooden playpens

Pros	Cons
• Arguably the most attractive style of pen, simply because it generally blends in better with other furnishings (remember that even though you will be able to fold the pen away, once it is up, it's likely to stay up for some time) • Usually has a larger floor area than other pens so more chance of it being popular with your baby	• Larger floor area also means it takes up more space and can dominate the room • Tends to be the most expensive type

Plastic playpens

Pros	Cons
• Wipe-clean and easy to maintain • Tends to be the least expensive type of 'permanent' pen	• Can be a garish-looking piece of equipment to have semi-permanently up in your home • Doesn't always have support to help your baby pull up from sitting

Fabric-sided playpens

Pros	Cons
• Cot or playpen – you choose what suits you when you need it • Can be folded for storage • One of the cheapest options	• These have mesh sides, which your baby can't see through as easily as bars, so may be less appealing • Lack of bars also means less support for pulling up from sitting, although some may have grab handles

> **!**
> • Don't put anything in the playpen that your baby can use as a lever or step to climb out.
> • Don't tie anything across the top as this could be a strangulation hazard.
> • Regularly check the pen for holes in the sides or in the floor padding.
> • Don't use the pen if it is damaged. Inspect it regularly.
> • Don't leave your child unattended in the pen unless you really have to.
> • Don't place the playpen near an open fire or other heat source.

Toilet training

The trials and tribulations of toilet training may seem a long way off but they will be with you before you know it. It's hard to say when is a good time to begin toilet training – each child is different and putting a child under pressure to use a potty when he or she isn't ready will put you both under unnecessary stress.

As a rough guide, a realistic time to start toilet training is at about two to two-and-a-half years old. Some parents start earlier if their child shows signs of interest, but 18 months is the earliest age to consider it. Years ago it was common practice to start toilet training at a far earlier stage than it is now (there are reports that at the beginning of the 20th century it was quite normal for the process to start at three months!). Parents and children then had practical reasons to toilet train as early as possible – with uncomfortable nappies (compounded by a lack of central heating) and poor washing facilities playing a large part. How long it took to complete the process is another matter altogether – starting early is no indication of the age at which a child will be fully toilet trained.

Thankfully, modern parents and babies have the luxury of being able to be more relaxed about the whole business. In practice, however, comparing progress with other parents and possibly being put under pressure by relatives and even nurseries or playgroups can cause toilet-training anxiety in even the most laid-back parents.

POTTIES

A potty is the standard item of toilet-training equipment. You'll need one or two of these. If you are new to potties, you might be surprised at the range of different types out there. Manufacturers just haven't been able to leave the standard potty alone on the shelf, and have come up with a plethora of potties (or 'toilet-training systems') with knobs on and prices to match. Not all the modern potty additions are gimmicks – some may appeal to you and to your child and could possibly help toilet training run more smoothly.

❝ You'll need one or two potties, which are available in a surprisingly wide range. ❞

Standard potties

These are simple, moulded pieces of plastic, usually with children's motifs on the front, a splash guard and a slightly raised back. Devoid of 'added extras', a basic potty may suit your needs cheaply and perfectly well.

Toilet-seat adaptors

Fitting on top of the main toilet seat, these adapt the seat so it is suitable for small bottoms. Generally they are made either from moulded rigid plastic, resembling the top section of a potty but with a rim to rest over the toilet seat (roughly the same price as a standard potty), or, for a comfier sit, from vinyl-covered padded material or with extras such as handles and a back-rest. If your child shows more of an interest in using the toilet than the potty, one of these could be worth a try.

Potty chairs

Basically a stubby chair with a central removable potty bowl, these provide more back and side support than a standard potty and may encourage some children to sit for longer.

Convertible/multi-use potties

These can be used as either a potty or, with the base section removed, as a toilet-seat adaptor. The base can usually also be used as a handy step-stool, making it easier for your child to climb on to the toilet. The main advantage of these potties is that they are versatile so adapt to the needs of your child at different stages. He or she can use the potty at the beginning of toilet training, the toilet-seat adaptor after further progress, and can carry on with the step-stool when using the toilet as normal but still needing an extra lift up. Extras may include a flip-up toilet-style lid to make the potty appear more grown-up.

Potty buying guide

- Make sure edges are gently curved for comfort and easy cleaning.
- Check that any removable parts can be slotted in and out easily (anything with a jerky movement could cause you to splash the waste).
- Think about where you will be washing the potty out – if your basin is on the small side, a bulky potty may be difficult to fit in to rinse properly, so choose a smallish potty or one with a removable interior.
- If you have a boy, check that the potty has a reasonably high 'splash guard' (a raised section at the front).
- Let your child choose the potty if possible – he or she will be keener to use it.
- Hold the potty to get a sense of how easy it will be to carry – you'll probably be carrying a full potty from room to room so will need easy-to-hold sides or handles.
- A high back can make it more comfortable if your child likes to use the potty as a sort of chair.

Portable/travel potties

Some children don't like using unfamiliar toilets or going to the toilet in unfamiliar places, such as the bushes in the park. Likewise, some parents would rather their child used their own potty or toilet-seat adaptor when out and about. A travel potty can be useful in these circumstances, and there are portable folding versions available.

TRAINING PANTS

When your child is showing clear signs that potty training is progressing well, you may want to introduce training pants into the process. They are not absolutely necessary and many parents progress straight from buying nappies to buying ordinary pants, with only a few accidents along the way. Training pants – particularly disposables – are, however, a popular toilet-training aid. The idea is that your child gets used to the action of pulling pants up and down when he or she wants to go to the toilet, but there is the added security of absorbent material in the pants, designed to cope with accidents.

There are two types of training pants – washable and disposable. Washable pants are more economical, especially if full toilet training seems to be dragging on. 'Luxury' washable training pants cost more but, since the idea is to use them

for a relatively short period of time, the extra expense seems unnecessary. Disposables are more convenient in that you don't have to do any washing, but they are more expensive than nappies.

The main disadvantage with this type of training pants, apart from the expense, is that some children can end up using them like nappies because they won't feel the discomfort of wetness in the way that children using the less absorbent washables will. There is therefore an argument that these can extend the toilet-training process rather than help to complete it. That said, many parents happily buy them because of their convenience.

Bear in mind that there is no point in using training pants before your child has a desire to use the potty or toilet and still seems unperturbed about 'soiling' him- or herself. You will be doing a lot of extra washing or spending extra money on disposable pants when this could be avoided.

❝While training pants are not absolutely necessary they can help ease the whole toilet-training process.❞

There are a few specialist nappy suppliers who also supply training pants via email. Go to www.bambinomio.com and www.twinkleontheweb.co.uk. Alternatively, scour your local supermarket for best buys.

PROTECTIVE BEDDING

Your child is quite likely to wet the bed once he or she stops using nappies at night. You'll want to be able to protect the mattress and change the bedding in the middle of the night quickly and easily. A range of protective sheets and covers is widely available both from nursery stores and department stores. Protective bedding has moved on from effective but uncomfortable, sweaty vinyl sheets (although you can still get these). More comfy bedding is multi-layered, with perhaps a vinyl layer but with softer, highly absorbent materials on top. A wet bed protection mat, as opposed to a protective sheet, can be very practical because it lies on top of a standard sheet so you can remove it without having to remake the bed.

Night-time training

When your child stops using nappies at night, keep at hand everything you will need to change the bedding in the middle of the night. Bear in mind that not only the sheet will be wet but also his or her nightclothes and possibly the quilt or blanket too. If you keep a spare set of everything close to your child's bed, disruption during the night will be minimised.

Toddler bathing

Bathtime can be one of the nicest times to share with your toddler, but it is also potentially the most dangerous because of the risks of drowning, scalding or slipping.

BATHING ACCESSORIES

No bathroom gathers clutter like that of a household with a toddler. In addition to the boatloads of toys, there are many accessories to keep your child happy while they get clean.

Bath rings

These are designed for babies who can sit unaided, so should only be used from around six months. They comprise a seat with an in-between-legs support, surrounded by a waist-height ring of plastic. Suction pads on the bottom attach to the main bath. The idea is that your baby stays sitting upright while being washed and can also play without moving around too much or slipping.

 There is a risk that bath rings may give parents a false sense of security and tempt them to pay less attention to their baby. Babies should never be left unattended in a bath, and be kept within arm's reach, no matter whether you are using a bath device or not.

❝A bath ring enables your baby to stay sitting upright and he or she can play without slipping.❞

The pros and cons of bath rings

Pros	Cons
• Keeps your baby in one place so you can wash him or her easily	• Active babies who want to play in the bath may find their movements restricted
• May help some babies feel more secure in the bath	• Some babies may struggle being put in the ring or it may be difficult to get them out

Non-slip bath mat

This is one of the few items of equipment you do genuinely need, once your baby starts sitting and pulling up without your support. Slippery babies and toddlers and a slippery bath could result in an accident. A bath mat provides a safe, non-slip surface. There are lots of bath mats designed specifically for children with fun designs on them, even with built-in thermometers. You will pay extra for these features, of course, and a standard bath mat will do the job perfectly well.

Unusual-shaped children's bath mats or bath appliqués (mini non-slip shapes often in the form of splashes or fishes) can be less effective because they may not cover as much of the bottom of the bath. For extra reassurance, a full-length bath mat can work well, particularly if you are bathing more than one child – these mats are fairly widely available.

Bath toy tidy

Plastic toys from all over the house will probably end up in the bath, and you will want to be able to tidy them and dry them quickly and easily. A bath toy tidy is a mesh bag that you attach with suction pads to the bathroom tiles above the bath. The mesh allows the water to drain away or air-dry easily, and the toys are always at hand to tip into the bath again. As your baby gets older, or you have more than one child in the bath, you may find that the bag isn't big enough to hold the range of toys that are required at bathtime, so you could end up with a collection perched around the bath edge or thrown into a box anyway. Regularly check the suction pads for any splits and breaks and if you find any, stop using it. Bath toy tidies are widely available from nursery stores.

Phthalates

Plastic material is often softened for uses, such as in toys, by chemicals called phthalates, which can be ingested by children placing the item in their mouth. Phthalates have been linked with causing kidney and testicle damage and cancer. Since January 2007, their use has been banned in products that can be placed in the mouth.

Shopping guide

This chapter has advice on where to look and buy, from local independents to massive retailers, including the numerous suppliers who are also online. Don't forget that buying or borrowing second-hand is often a good option and there is advice on checking second-hand goods on pages 197–9.

Where to shop

There is no shortage of retail outlets for baby products; the difficulty is more in deciding where to start. Your choice includes high-street chains and department stores, supermarkets, catalogue stores and small independent shops – as well as mail-order and online shopping.

There is no substitute for trying out major products like pushchairs for yourself before making a purchase. Do ask friends and other contacts for advice on products and suppliers, but don't buy solely on their recommendation because it may not be right for you. You may be able to 'road test' their equipment, which can be invaluable in identifying your own preferences.

The large retailers have websites giving details of their stock, which can be handy if you are looking for a specific style, and it is well worth browsing through their catalogues (which you can request online) because in addition to product information you can often get inspiration on how to decorate the nursery.

Fill your trolley

Your nearest major supermarket will probably be the best place for picking up essentials such as nappies, wipes and formula milk along with your regular shopping. Most produce their own lines, which are comparable in quality to the leading brands but better value for money.

LARGE NURSERY CHAIN STORES

There are three major nursery chains in the UK. Mothercare pioneered this market and is a major presence on the British high street, but two USA-based concerns also have stores around the country.

Babies 'R' Us

The specialist baby department of the US Toys 'R' Us chain, it has 70-odd stores around Britain. As well as baby toys, it offers just about everything else you might need – from nursery wardrobes to wipes. The full selection won't be available in every store but can be found in the catalogue or on the website (see page

> **❝When buying major products like pushchairs, there is no substitute for trying them out prior to buying. ❞**

Symbols on children's products

Although many parents recognise the symbols that are used on children's equipment and toys, they may not understand what each one represents.

Symbol	What it means
RESISTANT	• Will not easily catch light from cigarettes or matches • Does not mean fireproof
C E	• Manufacturer's self-declaration that its product meets basic EU legal requirements
(Kite mark)	• The Kite mark confirms that the British Standards Institution has tested a product and found it meets a particular standard
0-3	• Unsuitable for children under three years because it might, for instance, contain small parts
(Lion mark)	• The Lion mark shows that a toy meets British safety standards and adheres to strict advertising and counterfeiting ethics

204). The range is comparable to that of Mothercare and may be slightly cheaper. The main disadvantage is that because there are fewer stores you may not have the same opportunity to see and try out the products.

Mamas & Papas

A major nursery goods manufacturer that also has more than 30 stores around the country. Mamas & Papas only stocks its own-label products, but the range is extensive.

 This chapter is divided into different types of shops: see independent nursery stores on page 188, national chains on pages 189-91, and mail-order and online shopping on pages 191-3. Finally, there is guidance for internet research given on pages 194-5.

Shopping guide

Mothercare

This is the largest and probably the best-known nursery chain in the UK, with 230 stores. There are branches throughout the country, and a number of large, out-of-town stores called 'Mothercare World', which have a far wider range of stock than the town-centre shops. You can get more or less everything you need at Mothercare, the range is wide and the prices reasonable and the Mothercare own-label is especially good value. However, the store is not so good for more unusual items. You can order via the catalogue or the website, both of which offer a far more extensive range than in many of the high-street stores. You can apply for a Mothercare account card to help you spread the cost of payment.

Go online to shop local

One slightly different directory website is www.babydirectory.com – you click on your area on a map of the UK, and a local baby directory pops up. Click on the type of product you are interested in, e.g. 'Christening gowns', for contact details of relevant local shops.

INDEPENDENT NURSERY STORES

Faced with intense competition from the 'big players' in the nursery goods market, small independent nursery shops may not have quite the same drawing power they had for new parents in the past. However, your local independent nursery store could be one of the best places to go for one-to-one advice in an unhurried atmosphere. If you are served by the owner/manager or an experienced assistant, you may reap the benefits of talking to someone with plenty of knowledge of a wide range of nursery items and who will be prepared to spell out the pros and cons of various lines and brands.

The disadvantage is that, depending on the size of the store, you won't be able to view the same extensive range as in larger chain stores (although the shop may be able to order specific items for you). Price may also be an issue – independents won't have the 'value' own-brand lines that the main chain stores have, or the mass buying power.

Many independent nursery stores also have an online presence.

Look in your Yellow Pages under 'Baby Goods and Services', or Thomson Local directory under 'Baby and Nursery Equipment', to find out about nursery shops in your area.

 The contact details for all the stores described in this chapter are given in the Useful addresses section on pages 204-11.

NATIONAL CHAINS

In addition to the main nursery chains, there are smaller chains or department stores that have a good baby and toddler presence.

Adams This is a national chain selling own-label clothes for babies and children up to the age of 15. Adams clothes are also available in some Sainsbury's stores.

Argos This large store and catalogue retailer can be a good source of nursery equipment. It has outlets all over the country, and its nursery range includes most of the items you might be looking for, with major brand names represented – all at value-for-money prices. You can order at your local store, or from home via the catalogue or online.

Asda This supermarket offers a good selection of baby and children's clothing. A selection of larger Asda stores also contain a baby department, with car seats, pushchairs and other general nursery items. Bear in mind that shopping online can be useful for nappies and groceries when you have a small baby, and all of the main supermarkets offer this service.

BHS This department store has a good range of value-for-money baby and children's clothes.

Boots A high-street chain with a good reputation for feeding essentials (bottles, sterilisers and bibs, for example, as well as its own-brand baby food), in addition

Furniture and DIY stores

Big furniture stores often have children's bedroom ranges (but not cots), and you can get a fair selection of children's furnishings, including 'character' lamps and nursery wallpaper and borders, at the big DIY stores such as Homebase, Focus and B&Q.

to nappies and baby toiletries. Larger outlets also sell a decent selection of toys. As a general rule, stores tend to stock small rather than large items of baby equipment. However, you can order a wide selection of larger items from the Boots website or from the catalogue, available in stores.

Debenhams A national department store that stocks baby products, including clothing and pushchairs, and also operates online.

The Early Learning Centre stocks toys for babies and children. There are 215 Early Learning Centre stores across the UK and their goods are also sold in some Debenhams stores, Sainsbury's supermarkets and Boots.

Gap Sells upmarket baby clothing under the Baby Gap name.

H&M A national chain selling fashion clothing for all ages.

John Lewis Has a particularly good reputation for 'up-market' nursery

189

products as well as out-of-the-ordinary accessories and own-label and 'designer' baby clothes (although not all stores will stock the same items). Baby products and toys are listed on the website, and you can order online.

Ikea Worth a look for its range of nursery furniture – you can buy simply designed cots, changing tables, highchairs, wardrobes and chests of drawers, as well as toddler tables, chairs and beds (and lots of other practical baby products and toys), all at reasonable prices.

Marks & Spencer M&S stocks nursery items in some larger stores. You can choose from a small selection of car seats, pushchairs and cots, although this chain is stronger on baby clothes and nursery accessories such as bedding. Again, you can buy from the catalogue or online.

Loyalty schemes

Lots of retailers try to encourage customer loyalty for their baby goods by running baby club schemes, which give you money-off coupons on a range of products. Both Tesco and Babies 'R' Us, for example, reward those who join with a range of vouchers. Signing up also entitles you to free club magazines and mailings. Nappy manufacturers Pampers and Huggies also run their own clubs.

Department stores

Some department stores have excellent nursery departments. Although the ranges available may not be vast, many will have a good selection of quality products. It's worth paying a visit to your local department store to see what it can offer.

Matalan A 190-strong chain stocking clothing and household items that offers good, value-for-money baby and children's clothes and also sells online.

Next This clothing chain store offers a range of clothes for children from three months onwards.

Nippers Nippers is a small franchised chain that offers a wide range of baby products online and through a few stores stretched across the middle of the country.

Sainsbury's Sainsbury's has a deal with the Early Learning Centre (ELC) and Adams children's clothes so a range of ELC toys and Adams baby clothes are available in many of Sainsbury's stores.

Tesco Tesco stores offer a range of baby products and clothing, depending on the size of the store. This stock is also available online.

Woolworths Popular for value-for-money baby clothes, and larger branches have an excellent selection of well-known brand-name toys. Some branches also sell baby essentials such as nappies and wipes.

MAIL-ORDER AND ONLINE SHOPPING

All the retailers listed above also sell online. However, there are some specialist mail-order and online retailers who are worth investigating. Catalogue companies through which you can pay for goods by instalment may be worthwhile for the large and pricier items of equipment.

Ordering nursery items either by mail order or online certainly has its advantages. For one thing, you don't have to brave the shops with a baby in tow – you can browse the catalogues in the comfort of your home. Many of the mail-order and online nursery specialists have an interesting selection of products that you won't find in your local nursery store; the products are often sourced abroad and are introduced into the UK through these companies. If you are interested in something a bit out of the ordinary or are on the lookout for innovative ideas, there's a good chance of finding something to interest you in one of the specialist catalogues.

However, there are also disadvantages with buying in this way. The most obvious one is that you won't be able to see the goods before you buy or try them out in the way you can in a shop. This is particularly relevant when it comes to larger items such as pushchairs and cots – you can't, for example, test out how easy a pushchair is to fold or how smoothly the side of a cot slides down. You won't get the one-to-one attention or the demonstration of how to use a particular item that you may be offered in a high-street nursery store (although you can often get telephone advice). This drawback, of course, also applies to buying online or via mail order from one of the chain outlets. Bear in mind, too, that you usually have to pay for delivery.

If you decide a product isn't quite right for you or isn't what you were expecting once you have received it, you should be able to return it, but this can be a nuisance and you'll often have to pay the return postage costs. And if you associate catalogue shopping with relatively cheap prices, be warned that this doesn't necessarily apply to nursery catalogue specialists – many have quite an up-market feel and the products they sell and prices they charge tend to reflect this.

The contact details for all the stores described in this chapter are given in the Useful addresses section on pages 204-11.

Shopping guide

The Baby Catalogue sells a wide range of baby products including nappies, toys and furniture.

Baby Planet Tie-dye, hippy-chic baby and toddler clothes.

Beaming Baby Products with an environmentally friendly slant, including aromatherapy baby toiletries, organic cotton cuddly toys and bed linen, reusable nappies and a small selection of Fairtrade clothing.

Blooming Marvellous Maternity wear, including evening and professional outfits, plus accessories such as nursing bras, pregnancy support pillows and a device to listen to your unborn baby's heartbeat in the last few weeks; as well as nursery products and baby clothing (also has 'real world' shops).

Charlie Crow Imaginative dressing-up costumes for children aged 18 months to nine years.

Cheeky Rascals Practical products, including moulded, ergonomically designed feeding equipment, a good selection of travel equipment (with a wide choice of toddler 'buggy boards'), reusable nappies and a small selection of toys.

The Great Little Trading Company Extensive range of nursery furnishings and products, plus a large selection of indoor and outdoor toys and child-sized furniture. The Great Little Trading Company is also good for products for older children as well as for babies.

Green Baby Specialises in 'natural' baby products, including reusable nappies, organic cotton clothing and bedding, and wooden items from sustainable sources; the range is quite limited but unusual, and there are two 'real world' shops.

JoJo Maman Bébé Maternity wear plus nursery products, baby clothing, and lots of toys and storage products (also has 'real world' shops).

Kays This is a general catalogue retailer with a good selection of nursery products and you can pay over a period of a few months.

Kiddicare Stocks a wide range of well-known brands of nursery items, including pushchairs and car seats, many with good discounts.

Lilliput Offers a range of baby products online and has one large store in London.

Little Green Earthlets Reusable nappy specialists plus nursery goods with an environmentally friendly slant, including woollen clothing, non-endangered-species sea sponges for babies, unbleached cotton baby towels and bibs, and Merino wool blankets.

Littlewoods Has good-value baby and children's clothes and its website has a reasonable range of nursery items including cots and pushchairs.

Lullabys Has a store in Shropshire and additionally sells a wide range of baby goods online.

Mini Boden An off-shoot of clothing retailer Boden that offers stylish and practical baby and children's clothing, up to pre-teens.

Mischief Kids Sells designer clothes (including DKNY, Moschino and Miniman) for babies to teens.

Sugar Plum Tree offers exclusive and designer baby clothing.

Sunday Best Specialist in christening gowns, dresses and rompers.

Tiny Labels Sells designer baby clothes at discount prices.

Tomy manufactures a wide range of toys, sold online and nationally through many outlets.

Two Left Feet Offers a very wide range of baby products from its showroom in Milton Keynes and also sells online.

Urchin Out-of-the-ordinary furnishings, toys and practical products (for example, the 'spotty potty', fleece blankets with your baby's name embroidered on and pop-up travel cribs).

Vertbaudet A French catalogue company with a UK arm, also sells nursery items and has a large choice of baby, children's and maternity clothing.

❝ If you buy a product through mail order or online and decide it isn't quite right for you or isn't what you were expecting, you should be able to return it. ❞

Baby showers

This custom of holding a party for your baby either just before or after the birth - to which guests bring presents - is very big in the US and has some popularity in the UK. Some store and website retailers operate a baby shower gift list service along the same lines as a wedding list, so that presents are not duplicated. You could, if you want, just use it as a 'wish list' without going the whole hog and holding a party - after all, you'll be busy enough already!

GATEWAY SITES

There are some useful 'gateway' sites, which have links to retailers specialising in baby products. Many of those featured are small, independent businesses, and this can therefore be a useful way of locating more unusual products not available in the high-street shops (for example, handmade children's beds, softplay equipment and designer clothing). Three such are:

- www.babycentre.co.uk
- www.babyworld.co.uk
- www.all4kidsuk.com
- www.ukchildrensdirectory.com

Shopping directory sites that don't specialise in children's products will often still have a section relating to children – for example, try the 'Toys and Games' section of **www.topoftheshops. co.uk** for links to a number of toy retailer websites.

INTERNET RESEARCH

In addition to straightforward online shopping, the internet can be very handy if you are doing some general research, trying to track down a specific product, looking for the best deal, or how useful other parents have found a product to be.

There are also a number of parenting sites with 'chat rooms' or 'discussion forums' where you can ask other parents for information on their experiences of specific products. These can be a helpful source of independent viewpoints on items before you buy.

Product reviews

Some possibilities are Ciao, Shopzilla and Babyworld.

More general parents' discussion sites

These often offer very helpful advice and mention products that people find useful (or not). Some possibilities are the websites for:

- www.babycentre.co.uk
- *Mother and Baby* magazine: www.motherandbabymagazine.com
- Mothercare: www.mothercare.com
- ukparents.co.uk

❝ To locate more unusual products that aren't available in the high street, use specialised 'gateway' sites. ❞

The contact details for all the stores described in this chapter are given in the Useful addresses section on pages 204–11.

Getting the best price

If you know exactly what you want, you can also use the internet to help you shop around for the best deal on a product – particularly large items such as pushchairs and cots. Some nursery-product sites make a point of claiming that they will beat any other price. Others market themselves specifically as 'cut-price' outlets – **www.discountbabystore. co.uk**, for example, says that it sells all products at up to 50 per cent discount on recommended retail prices. Bear in mind that with such deals you may not get the latest models at big discounts, but you could well find a bargain on end-of-line and past-season goods.

Another option is to try an internet auction site. **www.ebay.co.uk** has an extensive 'Baby Items' section on its site, offering mostly second-hand clothes but also 'nearly new' pushchairs, nursery furniture and many other baby goods. Remember that if you are dissatisfied with the goods you buy from an auction site, because you are effectively buying from a private seller, your rights are more restricted than if you buy from an online or 'bricks and mortar' store.

❝Use websites that review products, and more general parent discussion sites to establish more information for items that you are interested in buying.❞

Buying toys

We've all seen the child who rejects the all-singing, all-dancing gift in favour of the box it came in, but actually a good toy can be a source of great joy and entertainment for all - except there are so many to choose from, so where do you start?

High-street stalwarts such as **Woolworths**, **Argos** and larger branches of **Boots** and **Mothercare** are excellent for good-value toys. **Ikea** also has a simple but appealing range. The toy departments at large department stores, independent toy shops and specialist toy chains, such as the **Early Learning Centre,** will have a more varied selection. Mail-order companies such as **Urchin** and the **Great Little Trading Company** also have interesting toy ranges. It is also worth looking at the websites or mail-order catalogues of the following specialist toy companies for more out-of-the-ordinary and innovative products.

Hamleys Lots of classic toys plus a reasonable selection of current ranges.

Krucial Kids Educational toys, particularly for pre-schoolers.

Letterbox Wide range of tasteful toys for babies and older children, including outdoor toys and a selection of unusual 'pop-up' and 'stacking' toys for babies.

Tridias Online branch of a small chain of toy shops selling quality toys from makes such as Galt and Brio. There is a refreshing absence of TV/cinema-themed products.

Toy libraries

Toy libraries are great for trying out a range of products on your child before committing to buying them. There are toy libraries all over the UK. The National Association of Toy and Leisure Libraries (NATLL) (www.natll.org.uk) can tell you where your nearest one is. It also produces an annual Good Toy Guide that gives awards for innovative and imaginative toy designs, and it rates toys according to their suitability for children with special needs.

Second-hand products

It makes a lot of sense to look for second-hand equipment and clothing. Clothes, in particular, are only used for a few months before they are outgrown and, similarly, some equipment is only needed for a relatively short time. So if you can safely avoid the expense of buying new, do so.

You might purchase second-hand products or, very commonly, have things given to you by friends and relatives who are only too pleased to pass on equipment and clothes that they no longer need. Parents who turn up their noses at hand-me-downs are missing out. Spare clothing is always useful – not until you have a baby do you realise quite how much clothing they can get through in a week or even a day. If you are offered equipment you're not sure you'll use, it's worth accepting and using it on a trial basis – you may find it indispensable or it may help to clarify what you really do need and would like to buy new.

Understandably, most parents want to buy new equipment such as a pushchair or a cot, which will be in use day-in, day-out for a couple of years or so. However, those items with a short lifespan that can be pricey to buy new, and with which there is no guarantee that they will suit your baby's needs or foibles, are good candidates for second-hand gifts or purchases. Examples of these are baby 'play' equipment, such as an automated swinging cradle or a baby bouncer (see pages 29–31 and 172–3). Moses baskets, cribs and carrycots can also be worth acquiring as hand-me-downs (see page 53), as they will only be in use for a few months or even weeks, until your baby moves into a cot (you may want to buy a new mattress for hygiene reasons but you need to make sure it fits correctly – see pages 56–60).

Some checks need to be undertaken to ensure that these products are safe as even though they may carry a BS safety mark (see list on page 187), over time they may be in a less safe condition. Also, you will be lucky to be given the instructions supplied when it was first purchased, which would have contained a lot of safety information.

❝If you can safely avoid the expense of buying new, do so.❞

Points to consider before buying: Second-hand items

The following general checklist should help you when looking at products:

Are there any areas of the product that appear to be damaged or badly worn? Check wooden areas to see if they are broken or splintered, metal bars for signs of bending and the seams or welds on fabric or plastic parts to see whether they are coming apart.

Have any modifications or repairs been made to the item? If so, the best advice is not to use it as you cannot vouch for its safety.

Has someone painted or varnished the item? If so, the finish may contain hazardous chemicals. If the product is looking scruffy, you may decide that it needs a coat of something, however, check with the supplier of the paint or varnish that what you intend using is safe for children.

If there are locks on the product to keep it in an unfolded position (such as pushchairs), check that these are sound and working properly. If products like travel cots or playpens that fold around a child are faulty, all of part of his or her body could be trapped, crushed or severed.

Check that any locks that are there to protect the child, such as on the drop sides of a cot or to secure a safety gate, are functioning correctly.

If the product has any internal padding, such as on a playpen or travel cot rim, check that the covering is intact. If a child gets any of the filling into his or her mouth, he or she could choke.

If there are any cords or ties on the product, make sure that they are less than 20cm (8in) long: any longer and they could get wound round the child's neck and strangle him or her.

Small parts that can be removed, pulled or broken off could be a choking hazard. Are there any sharp edges and corners or any protrusions that could penetrate an eye if a child fell on to them?

If the product has bars or slats, check that they are spaced no further apart than 6.5cm (2^1/$_2$in) to prevent the child slipping feet first between the bar and then becoming trapped by his or her neck, possibly causing strangulation.

The Child Accident Prevention Trust (CAPT) is a national charity committed to reducing the number of children and young people killed, disabled and injured as a result of accidents. To find out more, their website address is: www.capt.org.uk.

Where to look for second-hand products

Second-hand stores and charity shops are worth a browse for other 'nearly new' bargains. Some independent nursery shops have second-hand sections and some deal in just second-hand goods – these can be much better places to buy from as there is a good chance that you will be dealing with a sales assistant who knows about the equipment. It is also more likely that a product's condition will be checked before it is put on sale.

Local branches of the National Childbirth Trust (NCT) regularly organise 'Nearly New Sales' and these can be very useful sources of cheap equipment, clothes and toys, much of which will have had quite limited use. Visit the NCT's website for lists of sales in your area (www.nct.org.uk) or look out for adverts in local newspapers and shops. You could also try the 'Nearly New' section of www.netmums.com, a local information website for parents. The parent's discussion website www.ukparents.co.uk has a 'buy and sell' facility for trading second-hand items.

When you buy second-hand goods from a shop you have the same legal rights as when buying new. This means the goods must be fit for the purpose for which they're intended, including any purpose you made clear when purchasing, and must be of satisfactory quality. But the law also says that you must take into account the price you paid and be prepared to have lower expectations of quality than if the goods were new. You can also take goods back if there is a problem.

However, buying from car boot sales, auction sites, jumble sales or through the small ads is more of a risk. The Child Accident Prevention Trust advises parents not to buy equipment from these sources. If you choose to, the important thing is to satisfy yourself as far as possible that the product is safe, by observing the guidelines outlined above.

Jumble thinking

Jumble sales are great places for buying toys in particular. Prices are low so you can afford to experiment and make the odd mistake, and many of the toys are offered in good condition.

eBay

Many items on this popular auction website are second-hand. You can't inspect the products carefully over the internet and this will rule out purchases of items such as pushchairs and cots.

HIRING BABY EQUIPMENT

On some occasions you may need to hire equipment: either when on holiday, when you won't want to be over-burdened with luggage, or at home – perhaps if you have guests staying and need a spare cot, or if you know you will only be using an item (such as a baby swing) for a short time. Fortunately (particularly in holiday resorts) there are companies that hire out baby equipment, including pushchairs.

If you are staying in a holiday cottage organised via a letting agent, you will normally be able to hire cots and highchairs through the company. Sometimes these will be included in the cost of the cottage. If the agent itself doesn't deal with the baby equipment you want, it may be able to put you in touch with a local company that does. For more information on products you need for travelling with your baby, including on holiday, see pages 135–8. See also pages 197–9 for advice on checking out second-hand equipment.

You may find that your local independent nursery store has a 'for hire' section. If it doesn't, it should be able to put you in touch with a company that does. You could also look in your local Yellow Pages or Thomson Local directory – try under 'Baby Goods and Services' or 'Baby and Nursery Equipment' rather than 'Hire'. If there is a specialist hire company in your area, it should be listed in this section.

" There are occasions when being able to hire some equipment is useful. Look in your local Yellow Pages or Thomson Local directory under 'Baby Goods and Services' or 'Baby and Nursery Equipment'. "

Equipment for children and parents with special needs

If you have a child with special needs, you may need specialised equipment that is not available from standard shops.

Some equipment from mainstream manufacturers has particular uses for disabled children – for example, toilet-seat adaptors (see page 180) are helpful for children with balance and movement difficulties, according to the Research Institute for Consumer Affairs (RICA – see also Ricability below).

The Redinap Ezeechanger, a wall-mounted baby-changing unit, is marketed as being helpful for parents in a wheelchair or with bending or kneeling difficulties, because it can be attached to the wall at a comfortable height for whoever is using it.

The three-wheeler pushchair manufacturer, Baby Jogger, produces a special-needs version of the three-wheeler with a wider and deeper seat, which is available from Kidsense UK.

There are also many specialist retailers that cater for children with special needs. The following three organisations will be able to provide you with further information about these.

The Disabled Living Foundation, a charity with a particular interest in special-needs equipment, produces free and detailed fact sheets on a wide range of equipment that may be useful to parents of children with special needs. Three of these fact sheets – *Choosing children's daily living equipment, Choosing children's mobility equipment* and *Choosing children's play equipment* – are the most relevant and you can download them directly from the website (www.dlf.org.uk) or send an SAE to the address given on page 210. The website also has a discussion forum where participants exchange views or give advice on equipment.

Ricability publishes test reports on equipment for the disabled, including adults and children, from research carried out by the independent Research Institute for Consumer Affairs. There is a discussion forum on the website, and Ricability can answer queries if you want additional guidance on specific products.

Assist UK provides details of local Disabled Living Centres (there are 47 around the UK) where you can see and try out equipment and get advice on how to obtain it. Their website (www.assist-uk.org) has a search facility.

201

BSI numbers

Many of the products that you will need to buy will carry a British Standards Institution (BSI) number, which indicates that they comply with certain safety requirements, making them safe to use.

When purchasing a product check to see whether it is marked with either BS EN xxxx or BS xxxx followed by a date (the last four digits of the number). If this is not apparent – sometimes these numbers are hidden away – check with the person selling it whether there is a British Safety Standard for the particular item.

The following list gives those products where a safety standard exists.

Product	BSI number
Baby bouncers	BS EN 14036:2003
Baby walking frames	BS EN 1273:2005
Carrycots and stands	BS EN 1466:2004
Changing units	BS EN 12221:2000*
Child seats for cycles	BS EN 14344:2004
Children's bedguards	BS 7972:2001
Children's cots and folding cots	BS EN 716:1996 *
Children's harnesses, reins	BS EN 13210:2004
Children's pillows	BS 4578:1998
Cot bumpers	BS 1877-10:1997

Product	BSI number
Cribs and cradles	BS EN 1130
Cutlery and feeding utensils for children	BS EN 14372:2004
Drinking equipment for children	BS EN 14350:2004
Dummies for babies and young children	BS EN 1400:2002
Dummy holders	BS EN 12586:1999*
Fireguards	BS 8423:2002
Framed back carriers	BS EN 13209 Part 1:2004
Gates and safety barriers	BS EN 1930:2000*
Highchairs	BS EN 14988:2006
Inflatable armbands worn as floatation aids	BS 7661:1993
Mattresses for children's cots and prams	BS 1877-10:1997
Playpens	BS EN 12227:1999*
Portable child-appealing luminaries	BS EN 60598:2-10
Prams, pushchairs, buggies and travel systems	BS EN 1888:2003
Reclined cradles	BS EN 12790:2002*
Safety of children's clothing	BS EN 14682::2004
Safety of toys	BS EN 71
Soft carriers	BS EN 13209 Part 2:2005
Sun-safe clothing	BS 7949
Table-mounted chairs	BS EN 1272:1998
Travel cots	BS 7423: 1999

* Products that are currently under review and the date may change.

BSI numbers

203

Useful addresses

Large nursery chain stores

Babies 'R' Us
FREEPOST NAT 3362
Gateshead NE10 8BR
Tel (customer services): 0800 038 8889
www.babiesrus.co.uk

Mamas & Papas
Colne Bridge Road
Huddersfield
HD5 0RH
Tel: 0870 830 7700
www.mamasandpapas.co.uk

Mothercare
Mothercare Customer Service Centre
Cherry Tree Road
Watford
Hertfordshire WD24 6SH
Tel (customer services): 0845 330 4030
www.mothercare.co.uk

National chains

Adams
Tel: 024 7635 1000
adams.co.uk

Argos
Tel (customer services): 0870 600 8784
www.argos.co.uk

Asda
Tel (customer services): 0845 300 1111
(call to find out whether an Asda near you
has a George Babyshop)
www.asda.co.uk

B&Q
(Telephone nearest store for stock
information)
www.diy.com

BHS
Marylebone House
129–137 Marylebone Road
London NW1 5QD
Tel: 0845 196 00 00
www.bhs.co.uk

Boots
Tel (customer services): 0845 070 8090
www.boots.com

Debenhams
Debenhams Retail plc
1 Welbeck Street
London W1G 0AA
Tel (customer services): 08445 616161
www.debenhams.com

Early Learning Centre (ELC)
South Marston Park
Swindon SN3 4TJ
Orders:
Early Learning Direct
PO Box 4020
Manchester M99 1DA
Tel (customer services): 0870 535 2352
www.elc.co.uk

Gap
Head Office
Berkley Square House
London W1J 5BS
Tel: 01788 818300
www.gap.com

H&M
Head Office
Holden House
57 Rathbone Place
London W1N 9LB
Tel: 020 73232211
www.hm.com

Homebase
Tel (customer services): 0845 077 8888
www.homebase.co.uk

John Lewis
Tel (customer services): 0845 604 9049
www.johnlewis.com

Ikea
(Telephone nearest store for stock information)
www.ikea.co.uk

Marks and Spencer
Tel (customer services): 0845 302 1234
www.marksandspencer.co.uk

Matalan
Tel: 0845 330 7330
www.matalan.co.uk

Next
Head Office
Desford Rd
Enderby
Leicester LE19 4AT
Tel: 0845 600 7000
next.co.uk

Nippers
Little Porters
Porters Lane
Fordham Heath
Colchester CO3 9TZ
Tel: 0870 067 5434
www.nippers.co.uk

Sainsbury's
Head Office
33 Holborn, London EC1N 2HT

Tel (customer services): 0800 636262
www.sainsburys.com

Tesco
Tel (customer services): 0800 505555
www.tesco.com

Woolworths
Woolworth House
242–246 Marylebone Road
London NW1 6JL
Tel: 020 7262 1222
www.woolworths.co.uk

Mail order and online shopping

The Baby Catalogue
Perfectly Happy People Ltd
90 Bollo Lane
Chiswick
London W4 5LU
Tel: 0870 120 2018
www.thebabycatalogue.com

Baby Planet
60 Melbourne Road
Clacton-on-Sea
Essex CO15 3HZ
Tel: 0870 345 0526
www.baby-planet.co.uk

Beaming Baby
Unit 1
Place Barton Farm
Moreleigh
Totnes
Devon TQ9 7JN
Tel: 0800 034 5672
www.beamingbaby.com

Blooming Marvellous
2nd Floor
1 The Broadway
Surbiton KT6 7DQ
Tel: 0845 458 7408
www.bloomingmarvellous.co.uk

Charlie Crow
Unit 2
Crabtree Close, Fenton
Stoke-on-Trent ST4 2SW
Tel: 01782 417133
info@charliecrow.co.uk
www.charliecrow.com

Cheeky Rascals
Tel: 0870 873 2600
www.cheekyrascals.co.uk

The Great Little Trading Company
Pondwood Close
Moulton Park
Northampton NN3 6DF
Tel (customer services): 0870 850 6000
www.gltc.co.uk

Green Baby
Unit 2Q/R, Leroy House
436 Essex Rd
London N1 3QP
Tel: 0870 241 7661
www.greenbabyco.com

JoJo Maman Bébé
Tel: 0870 160 8820
info@jojomamanbebe.co.uk
www.jojomamanbebe.co.uk

Kays
Head Office
Thynne Street
Bolton BL78 1BH
Tel: 0870 151 0541
enquiry@kays.com
www.kaysnet.com

Kiddicare
1182 Lincoln Road
Werrington
Peterborough PE4 6LA
Tel: 01733 579175
www.kiddicare.com

Lilliput
255 Queenstown Road
London SW8 3NP
Tel: 020 7720 5554
www.lilliput.com

Little Green Earthlets
Units 17
Silveroak Farm
Waldron
Heathfield
East Sussex TN71 0RS
Tel: 0845 072 4462
www.earthlets.co.uk

Littlewoods
Tel (customer services): 08457 888 222
www.littlewoods.com

Lullabys
Coton Hill
Shrewsbury SY1 2DP
Tel: 01743 367994
sales@lullabys.co.uk
www.lullabys.co.uk

Mini Boden
Customer Services:
Boden
Meridian West
Meridian Business Park
Leicester LE19 1PX
Tel: 0845 677 5000
www.boden.co.uk

Mischief Kids
20 Market Street
Leigh
Lancashire WN7 1DS
Tel: 01942 607222
www.mischiefkids.co.uk

Sugar-plum Tree
29 East Street
Ilminster
Somerset TA19 0AN
Tel: 01460 259259
sales@sugar-plumtree.co.uk
www.sugar-plumtree.co.uk

Sunday Best
115 Adnitt Road
Northampton NN1 4NQ
Tel: 01604 639 229
www.sundaybest.com

Tiny Labels
The Carriages
Kemberton
Shifnal
Shropshire TF11 9LH
Tel: 01952 585640 (7–9pm)
www.tiny-labels.co.uk

Tomy
PO Box 20, Totton
Hampshire SO40 3YF
Tel: 023 8066 2600 (call for details of product stockists)
www.tomy.co.uk

Two Left Feet
Tel: 01234 867777
www.twoleftfeet.co.uk

Urchin
Freepost SCE 6264
Marlborough, Wiltshire SN8 3YY
Tel: 0870 112 6006
www.urchin.co.uk

Vertbaudet
PO Box 125
Bradford BD99 4YG
Tel: 0870 050 2120
www.vertbaudet.co.uk

Buying toys

Hamleys
188–196 Regent Street
London W1R 6BT
Tel: 0800 2802 444
www.hamleys.co.uk

Krucial Kids
Unit 11
Enterprise Way
Flitwick
Bedfordshire MK45 5BW
Tel: 01525 722740
www.krucialkids.com

Letterbox
Tregony Business Park
Tregony
Truro
Cornwall TR2 5TL
Tel: 0870 066 7676
www.letterbox.co.uk

Tridias
The Buffer Depot
Badminton Road
Acton Turville
Gloucestershire GL9 1HE
Tel: 0870 443 1300
www.tridias.co.uk

Manufacturers of specific products

Bambino Mio
(*Nappies*)
12 Stavely Way
Brixworth
Northampton NN6 9EU
Tel: 01604 883777
www.bambinomio.co.uk

The Better Baby Sling
47 Brighton Road
Watford WD24 5HN
Tel: 01923 444442
www.betterbabysling.co.uk

Birth Works
(*Birthing pools to buy or hire*)
Tel: 020 8244 9785
www.birthworks.co.uk

Clippasafe
Lanthwaite Road
Clifton
Nottingham NG11 8LD
Tel: 0115 921 1899 (call for details of product stockists)
www.clippasafe.co.uk

Cotton Bottoms
(*Re-usable nappies*)
www.tommeetippee.co.uk

Graco
(*Various products*)
1st Floor
900 Pavilion Drive
Northampton NN4 7RG
Tel: 0870 909 0501 (call for details of product stockists)
www.graco.co.uk

Grobag
(*Baby sleeping bags*)
Gro-group UK Ltd
Unit C4

Linhay Business Park
Ashburton TQ13 7UP
Tel: 0870 420 4920
www.grobag.com

Halfords
Tel (customer services): 08450 579 000
www.halfords.com
(for safety reasons car seats can only be bought in-store, although they can be viewed online)

Huggababy
(*Baby carriers and other baby related products*)
Cannon Business Park
Gough Road
Coseley
Wolverhampton
West Midlands WV14 8XR
Tel: 08700 053156
www.huggababy.co.uk

Jack Horner Cot Company
PO Box 1448
Rugby CV23 8ZE
Tel: 01788 891890 (call for details of product stockists)
www.jack-horner.co.uk

Jané
Johnston Prams and Buggies Ltd
Unit 6 Trench Park
Trench Road, Mallusk
Newtonabbey BT36 4TY
Tel: 028 9084 9045
www.johnstonprams.co.uk

Kidsense
(*Strollers and buggies*)
Foxlands Farm
Croft Road
Leicestershire LE9 1SG
Tel: 0116 2751895
www.kidsense.co.uk

Lindam
(*Various*)
Hornbeam Square West
Hornbeam Park
Harrogate
North Yorkshire HG2 8PA
Tel: 08701 118 118 (call for details of
product stockists)
www.lindam.com

The Natural Mat Company
(*Mattresses and other baby products*)
99 Talbot Road
London W11 2AT
Tel: 020 7985 0474
www.naturalmat.com

Rabbitts
(*Safety harness changing mat*)
99 Park Street Lane
Park Street
St Albans
Hertfordshire AL2 2JA
Tel: 01727 875747
www.rabbitts.com

Redinap
(*Nappy changing units*)
PO Box 6632
Birmingham B37 6DD
Tel: 0121 788 0300 (call for details of
product stockists)
www.redinap.com

Silver Cross
(*Prams and travel systems*)
Nesfield House
Broughton Hall
Skipton
North Yorkshire BD23 3AN
Tel: 01756 702412
www.silvercross.co.uk

Snugger
(*Sleeping bags for babies*)
PO Box 570

Cheam
Sutton
Surrey SM2 7LE
Tel: 020 8224 8766
www.snuggeruk.com

Splashdown Water Birth Services Ltd
(*National birth pool hire*)
17 Wellington Terrace
Harrow on the Hill
Middlesex HA1 3EP
Tel: 08456 123405
www.waterbirth.co.uk

Starchild
(*Shoes for babies and children*)
Unit 17/18
Oak Business Centre
Ratcliffe Road
Sileby
Leicester LE12 7PU
Tel: 01509 817600 (order line)
www.starchildshoes.co.uk

Stokke
(*Various, including high chairs and cots*)
Customer services: info.uk@stokke.com
www.stokke.com

Twinkle Twinkle
(*Nappies*)
Linpac Building
Headley Road East
Woodley
Reading RG5 4HY
Tel: 0118 969 5550
Nappy advice:
nappyhelp@twinkleontheweb.co.uk
www.twinkleontheweb.co.uk

UK Nappy Line
Tel: 01983 401959
www.realnappy.com

Wilkinet
(*Baby carrier*)
P.O. Box 4521
Southam
CV47 4AS
Tel: 0800 2550 247
www.wilkinet.co.uk

Associations and support groups

Assist UK
Redbank House
4 St Chad's Street
Manchester M8 8QA
Tel: 0870 770 2866
www.assist-uk.org

British Toy and Hobby
Association
80 Camberwell Road
London SE5 OEG
Tel: 020 7701 7271
www.btha.co.uk

Child Accident Prevention Trust
4th Floor
Cloister Court
22–26 Farringdon Lane
London EC1R 3AJ
Tel: 020 7608 3828
www.capt.org.uk

Northern Ireland
23A/B Mullacreevie Park
Killylea Road
Armagh BT60 4BA
Tel: 028 3752 6521
www.capt.org.uk

Disabled Living Foundation
380–384 Harrow Road
London W9 2HU
Tel: 020 7289 6111 (enquiries,
9am–5pm)
Helpline: 0845 130 9177
www.dlf.org.uk

Food Standards Agency (FSA)
Aviation House
125 Kingsway
London WC2B 6NH
Tel: 020 7276 8000
www.food.gov.uk

Foundation for the Study of Infant
Deaths (FSID)
Artillery House
11–19 Artillery Row
London SW1P 1RT
Helpline: 020 7233 2090
General: 020 7222 8001
www.fsid.org.uk

La Leche League
PO Box 29
West Bridgford
Nottingham NG2 7NP
Helpline: 0845 120 2918
Enquiries: 0845 456 1855 (Mon and
Thurs)
www.laleche.org.uk

National Association of Nappy Services
(NANS)
(call the number below for postal address of
the current chair of NANS)
Tel: 0121 693 4949
www.changeanappy.co.uk

National Association of Toy and Leisure
Libraries (NATLL)
68 Churchway
London NW1 1LT

Tel: 020 7255 4600
www.natll.org.uk

Scotland office
1st Floor
Gilmerton Community Centre
4 Drum Street
Edinburgh EH17 8QG
Tel: 0131 664 2746
www.natll.org.uk

Wales office
Steeple House
Steeple Lane
Brecon
Powys LD3 7DJ
Tel: 01874 622 097
www.natll.org.uk

National Childbirth Trust (NCT)
Alexandra House
Oldham Terrace
Acton
London W3 6NH
Tel: 0870 444 8707
Breastfeeding line: 0870 444 8708
Pregnancy and birth line: 0870 444 8709
www.nct.org.uk

Ricability
(*reports on products for disabled children*)
30 Angel Gate
326 City Road
London EC1V 2PT
Tel: 020 7427 2460
www.ricability.org.uk

Useful websites

Gateway sites
www.all4kidsuk.com
www.babycentre.co.uk
www.babydirectory.com
www.babyworld.co.uk
www.ukchildrensdirectory.com

Product reviews
www.babyworld.co.uk
www.ciao.co.uk
www.shopzilla.co.uk
www.which.co.uk

Discussion sites
www.motherandbabymagazine.com
www.netmums.com
www.ukparents.co.uk

Safety
www.childcarseats.org.uk
www.rospa.com

Travelling with children
www.babygoes2.com
www.travellingwithchildren.co.uk

Index

Index

which?

Which? is the leading independent consumer champion in the UK. A not-for-profit organisation, we exist to make individuals as powerful as the organisations they deal with in everyday life. The next few pages give you a taster of our many products and services. For more information, log onto www.which.co.uk or call 0800 252 100.

Which? magazine
Which? is, quite simply, the most trusted magazine in the UK. It takes the stress out of your buying decisions by offering independent, thoroughly researched advice on consumer goods and services from cars to current accounts via coffee makers. Its Best Buy recommendations are the gold standards in making sound and safe purchases across the nation. Which? has been making things happen for all consumers since 1957 – and you can join us by subscribing at www.which.co.uk or calling 0800 252 100 and quoting 'Which'.

Which? online
www.which.co.uk gives you access to all Which? content online. Updated daily, you can read hundreds of product reports and Best Buy recommendations, keep up to date with Which? campaigns, compare products, use our financial planning tools and interactive car-buying guide. You can also access all the reviews from the *The Which? Good Food Guide*, ask an expert in our interactive forums, register for e-mail updates and browse our online shop – so what are you waiting for? www.which.co.uk.

Which? Legal Service
The Which? Legal Service offers immediate access to first-class legal advice at unrivalled value. One low-cost annual subscription allows members to enjoy unlimited legal advice by telephone on a wide variety of legal topics, including consumer law (problems with goods and services), employment law, holiday problems, neighbour disputes and parking/speeding/clamping issues. Our qualified lawyers help members reach the best outcome in a user-friendly way, guiding them through each stage on a step-by-step basis. Call 0800 252 100 for more information or visit www.which.co.uk.

which?

Which? Books

Other books in this series

The Tax Handbook 2007/8
By Tony Levene
ISBN: 978 1 84490 039 8
Price £10.99

Make sense of the complicated rules, legislation and red-tape with the *Tax Handbook 2007/8*. Written by Guardian finance journalist and tax expert Tony Levene, this essential guide gives expert advice on all aspects of the UK tax system and does the footwork for you. It includes information on finding the right accountant and how to get the best from them, advice on NI contributions, tax credits for families and the self-assessment form. An indispensable guide for anyone who pays tax.

The Pension Handbook
By Jonquil Lowe
ISBN: 978 1 84490 025 1
Price £10.99

A definitive guide to sorting out your pension, whether you're deliberating over SERPs/S2Ps, organising a personal pension or moving schemes. Cutting through confusion and dispelling apathy, Jonquil Lowe provides up-to-date advice on how to maximise your savings and provide for the future.

Giving and Inheriting
By Jonquil Lowe
ISBN: 978 1 84490 032 9
Price £10.99

Inheritance tax (IHT) is becoming a major worry for more and more people. Rising house prices have pushed up the value of typical estates to a level where they are liable to be taxed at 40% on everything over £285,000. *Giving and Inheriting* is an essential guide to estate planning and tax liability, offering up-to-the–minute advice from an acknowledged financial expert, this book will help people reduce the tax bill faced by their heirs and allow many to avoid IHT altogether.

which?

Which? Books

Other books in this series

Divorce and Splitting Up

By Imogen Clout
ISBN: 978 1 84490 034 3
Price £10.99

Divorce, separation, dissolution of a civil partnership or simply splitting up with a partner is never easy – the emotional upheaval, legal complexities and financial implications make even the most amicable parting a demanding business; when children are involved, couples are in dispute and property needs to be divided the whole process can be fraught with difficulties. *Divorce and Splitting Up* offers comprehensive, clear, step-by-step guidance through the whole process, explaining how the law works, drawing attention to key considerations and looking at ways of minimising unnecessary conflict and costs.

What To Do When Someone Dies

By Paul Harris
ISBN: 978 1 84490 028 2
Price £10.99

Coping with bereavement is never easy but this book makes dealing with the formalities as straightforward and simple as possible. Covering all the practicalities, this book provides step-by-step guidance on registering a death, making funeral arrangements, applying for probate and sorting out the financial matters.

Wills and Probate

By Paul Elmhirst
ISBN: 978 1 84490 033 6
Price £10.99

Wills and Probate provides clear, easy-to-follow guidance on the main provisions to make in a will and the factors you should consider when drafting these. The second part of the book provides step-by-step guidance on probate, making the process as straightforward and trouble-free as possible. By being aware of key changes and revisions and avoiding the problems and pitfalls, you can limit delays, avoid disputes and save tax.

which?

Which? Books

Other books in this series

Buy, Sell and Move House

By Kate Faulkner
ISBN: 978 1 84490 030 5
Price £10.99

A complete, no-nonsense guide to negotiating the property maze and making your move as painless as possible. From dealing with estate agents to chasing solicitors, working out the true cost of your move to understanding Home Information Packs, this guide tells you how to keep things on track and avoid painful sticking points.

Renting and Letting

By Kate Faulkner
ISBN: 978 1 84490 029 9
Price £10.99

A practical guide for landlords, tenants, and anybody considering the buy-to-let market. Covering all the legal and financial matters, including tax, record-keeping and mortgages, as well as disputes, deposits and security, this book provides comprehensive advice for anybody involved in renting property.

Buying Property Abroad

By Jeremy Davies
ISBN: 978 1 84490 024 4
Price £10.99

A complete guide to the legal, financial and practical aspects of buying property abroad. This book provides down-to-earth advice on how the buying process differs from the UK, and how to negotiate contracts, commission surveys, and employ lawyers and architects. Practical tips on currency deals and taxes – and how to command the best rent – all ensure you can buy abroad with total peace of mind.

Which? Books

Which? Books provide impartial, expert advice on everyday matters from finance to law, property to major life events. We also publish the country's most trusted restaurant guide, *The Which? Good Food Guide*. To find out more about Which? Books, log on to www.which.co.uk or call 01903 828557.

" Which? tackles the issues that really matter to consumers and gives you the advice and active support you need to buy the right products. "